my first
POMPOM
BOOK

my first POMPOM BOOK

35 fantastic and fun crafts for children aged 7+

LUCY HOPPING

CICO Kidz

Published in 2017 by CICO Kidz

An imprint of Ryland Peters & Small Ltd

20–21 Jockey's Fields, London WC1R 4BW

341 E 116th St, New York, NY 10029

www.rylandpeters.com

10 9 8 7 6 5 4 3 2 1

A CIP catalog record for this book is available from the
Library of Congress and the British Library.

ISBN: 978 1 78249 444 7

Printed in China

Series consultant: Susan Akass
Editor: Katie Hardwicke
Designer: Alison Fenton
Illustrator: Hannah George
Template illustrations: Stephen Dew

In-house editor: Dawn Bates
In-house designer: Fahema Khanam
Art director: Sally Powell
Head of production: Patricia Harrington
Publishing manager: Penny Craig
Publisher: Cindy Richards

For photography credits, see page 128

Contents

Introduction

What is nicer than a pompom? Even the name is fun to say and every pompom is fun to make, and adds a cute and playful touch to whatever it is used for. Wind yarn, cut, tie, and out pops a soft fluffy 3-D ball—it's magical!

My First Pompom Book is full of ideas about things to make with pompoms, from weird and wacky birdies to soft cuddly dinosaurs, from a cute mobile of little lambs to pretty angels to top off your Christmas tree. Most of the pompoms are made with yarn (wool) but other materials are used too, such as tissue paper to make the paper pompoms which are the must-have accessory for your cheerleading routines. The projects use pompoms in different sizes, including tiny readymade craft pompoms and felt balls, and there are even some ideas for using pretty pompom trim, so that you can get that fun effect in an instant!

My First Pompom Book is divided into four chapters. Chapter One, Pompom Creatures, brings you a wonderful collection of adorable pompom pets. If you haven't got a rabbit or a kitten, here's your chance to make one! Chapter Two shows you how to use pompoms in all your seasonal celebrations from Halloween to Easter, and gives you some fun ideas for parties, too. The third chapter brings you fun and stylish pompom accessories—how about making a funky poodle phone case, or a pretty bangle from ready-made pompom trim? Finally, in Chapter Four you'll discover beautiful decorations to give as gifts or for making your own room extra special—try a hanging heart or paper flowers strung from invisible thread.

Before you begin, look through the techniques section, which tells you exactly how to make pompoms and any other techniques you need to complete the projects. As you are going to be making a lot of pompoms, it may be worth buying a set of plastic pompom maker tools as these are much quicker than the traditional way of using rings of cardboard. There are several different types, which come with their own instructions, but all follow the same basic technique—wind, cut, and tie. If you haven't got a plastic tool, no problem. We have included templates to make cardboard ones that work just as well. We also show you how to make mini pompoms using a fork! Check the suggested list of materials so that you can get started whenever you feel the need to make another pompom.

To help you plan your crafting, we have graded the projects with one, two, or three smiley faces. Level one projects are the easiest with simple pompom making, a little cutting, and sticking. Level two projects take a bit longer—there will be more pompoms to make and join, and a few other craft skills to finish the projects. Level 3 projects are the most challenging—they are longer projects that involve some more complicated crafting techniques but are well worth the effort.

So, what are you waiting for? Get winding that yarn for your first fluffy pompom!

Project levels

◕○○

Level 1
These are quick and simple projects.

◕◕○

Level 2
These projects take a little longer and involve making and shaping different-size pompoms and other craft skills.

◕◕◕

Level 3
These projects are more challenging and may require some help, and will take a little longer.

Getting Started

For all the projects it is useful to have these basic materials in your crafting kit. For some projects you may need to find or buy some special materials. Check the "You will need" list before you begin.

Basic equipment
Yarn (wool) in lots of different colors
Pencils
Ruler
Pencil sharpener
Erasers
Felt-tipped pens
Acrylic paints
Thick and thin paintbrushes
Palette or plate for mixing paint
Water pot or jar
Pair of sharp scissors with pointed ends
Glue stick
White (PVA) craft glue and spreader
Sticky tape and double-sided sticky tape
Sticky tack
Paper clips
Hole punch
Stapler

Craft materials
Pompom makers in different sizes
Mini craft pompoms in different sizes and colors
Craft popsicle (lolly) sticks
Googly eyes
Craft foam sheets
Felt sheets
Pipe cleaners
Glitter
Washi tape or decorative masking tape

Paper and card
Cardboard packaging for making pompom rings (cereal boxes are ideal)
White and colored paper
White and colored card
Colored tissue paper
Patterned paper or gift wrap
Tracing paper
Squared math paper
Old newspapers and magazines (ask first before you cut them up!)

Sewing stash
Yarn needle with a large eye
Needle threader
Sewing needles and thread
Pins
Fabric scissors
Embroidery floss (thread) and needle
Invisible thread
Ribbons and braid
Pompom trim
Beads—some with big holes
Old T-shirts
Buttons and beads
Sequins

Craft Techniques

There are many ways to make pompoms, but here we show you how to make a classic yarn pompom. The choice of yarn is important—try variegated yarns for multicolored effects, fluffy yarn for cute creatures, or even fabric and netting.

Standard pompom sizes

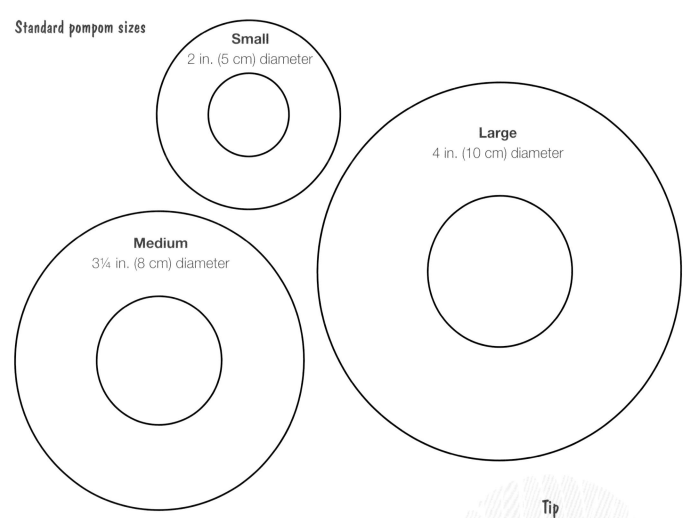

Small
2 in. (5 cm) diameter

Large
4 in. (10 cm) diameter

Medium
3¼ in. (8 cm) diameter

Pompoms are made by wrapping yarn or other materials around the rings of a pompom maker. You can make your own from cardboard or you could buy a pompom maker tool from the craft store. These are available in different sizes—look for one that has several size options. We have used cardboard rings in small, medium, and large. Copy these ring templates, or make your own by drawing a circle to the diameter that you would like your pompom to be, remembering to cut a hole in the center and to cut out two circles of cardboard.

Tip
It can be quite difficult to thread very thick yarn or fabric through the holes as they fill up quickly. Instead, cut a small section away from the ring before you start wrapping (see Snowball template on page 124).

Using a cardboard pompom maker

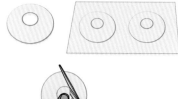

1 Trace the pompom ring templates onto card and cut out two rings. Cut out the hole in the center.

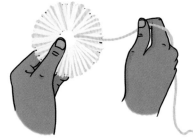

2 Cut a length of yarn about 2.2 yd (2 m) long and wind it into a loose ball that will fit through the middle hole of the ring. Hold the cardboard rings together and begin to wrap the yarn around the cardboard, pushing it through the center hole and back over the outside.

3 Keep winding the yarn around the ring, pulling it through until the whole ring is covered. When you reach the end of the yarn, cut another length, tie it to the first length, and continue to wind the yarn. Build up layers of yarn all the way round the rings until there is no more room in the middle to push the yarn through (you can thread the end onto a needle to help). The more layers there are, the fluffier the pompom.

4 Now, holding the pompom rings firmly together, push one blade of a pair of scissors through the yarn and between the card rings. Cut the yarn all around the edge of the rings— this is quite hard work! Hold the rings together as you cut.

5 Cut a length of yarn about 8 in. (20 cm) long. Hold one end in one hand and thread the other end between the two card rings. Wind it round tightly twice and then tie the two ends together in a tight knot.

6 Gently pull the card rings away from the pompom. If this is difficult, you could cut them off but then you can't reuse them to make more pompoms! Trim any strands of yarn that are too long, taking care to leave the tying ends long if they are needed later in the instructions, and fluff up your pompom. All done!

Using a plastic pompom maker tool

There are several brands of pompom makers but many follow the same style of a split ring, with two plastic hinged rings that clip together. Because each half is wound separately and you don't have to push the yarn through the center, they are much quicker to use than card rings.

1 Clip the two halves together at one end. With the rings open, start wrapping the yarn 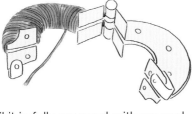 around one half until it is fully covered with several layers of yarn, and the center is full. Cut the yarn, leaving a long end.

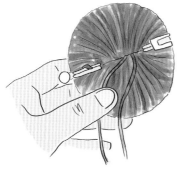

2 Do the same on the other half of the tool, wrapping the yarn until it is full. Clip the two halves of the ring together.

3 Insert the open blade of a pair of scissors between the rings and snip the strands around the whole ring. Tie a long length of yarn around the middle, wrap it around two or three times, then knot it tightly.

4 Unclip the two halves and remove the plastic rings. Trim and fluff up your pompom, taking care to leave the tying ends long if they are needed later in the instructions.

Making pompoms with a fork

Use this method to make mini pompoms—it's really quick and easy and you can make a whole batch of cute pompoms all in one go.

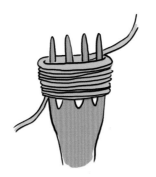

1 Cut a length of yarn about 3 yd (3 m) long. Wrap the yarn around the tines (prongs) of a metal fork until you have used up the entire length.

2 Cut a length of matching yarn about 8 in. (20 cm) long. Thread one end of the yarn through the middle prongs of the fork at the bottom, beneath the wrapped strands. Tie the ends around the wrapped strands very tightly and knot in place (see Tying a reef knot, page 15).

3 Slide the yarn bundle off the fork, wrap the ends of the tie around the middle again, and tie another knot. Slide the open blades of a pair of scissors through the loops of yarn and cut the strands. Do the same on the other side.

4 Fluff up the mini pompom and trim any long ends to make a neat ball, taking care to leave the tying ends long if they are needed later in the instructions.

Tying pompoms together

Some projects use two or more pompoms tied together to make a larger shape. You can do this by using the long ends of the yarn that were tied between the card rings. Always check the instructions to make sure that you leave these long when you trim your pompom if necessary.

1 Take the two ends from both pompoms and tie them in a knot (see Tying a reef knot, page 15).

2 To add extra pompoms, thread one long tying end onto a yarn needle, feed it through the center of the pompom,

and out on the side where you would like to join the next pompom. Do the same with the second tying thread, then tie the pompoms together as in step 1.

Copying templates

For some of the projects you need to copy a template from the back of the book, cut it out, and draw around it. You can trace some of the templates onto white paper or you can photocopy them onto paper or thin card. Some templates have to be enlarged and these ones will need to be photocopied—follow the percentage enlargement given with the template. For some projects you will need to use tracing paper to transfer details from a template. This is how you use it.

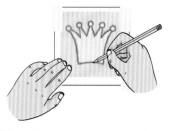

1 Place a sheet of tracing paper over the template and hold it in place with masking tape. Trace the lines with a hard 4 (2H) pencil.

2 Turn the tracing paper over so that the back is facing you and neatly scribble over the lines with a softer pencil, such as a 2 (HB).

3 Turn the paper over again so that the top is facing you and position it on your paper or card (use masking tape to hold it in place). Draw over the lines you made in step 1 with the hard pencil, then remove the tracing paper. This will transfer the pencil to give you a nice, clear outline.

Making a bow

A bow is a lovely way to finish your pompom project, so here are some simple instructions to help you to tie the perfect bow.

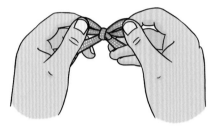

1 Make a loop in the ribbon and wrap the other end of the ribbon around, as if tying your shoelace.

2 Push another loop of ribbon through the circle of ribbon you have just made around the first loop. Tighten both loops to make a bow.

3 Adjust the ends until your bow is neat and symmetrical.

Braiding (plaiting)

This is a great way to make a length of cord to attach a pompom to one end.

1 Knot three equal pieces of yarn together at one end. Hold the knotted end firm with a clip, stick it down with some tack, or pin it to a pillow (cushion) with a safety pin (or ask someone to hold it for you).

2 Take the right strand of yarn over the middle strand— this then becomes the middle strand.

3 Take the left strand over the middle strand—this then becomes the middle strand.

4 Keep repeating right over middle, left over middle, until you reach the end. Tie the strands together in a knot.

Tying a reef knot

This is a strong knot to tie two pieces of yarn together, when tying pompoms together for example, or to tie two ends together to make a hanging loop.

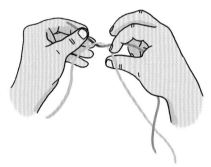

1 Take the left end of the yarn, pass it across the right end, and twist it underneath.

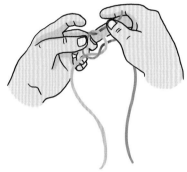

2 The ends have now swapped places. Take what has now become the right end and pass it over the left end, twist it underneath, and bring it up through the loop you have just made.

3 Now pull all the ends tight.

4 This little rhyme will help you remember: "Left over right and under, right over left and under."

Sewing Techniques

Some of the pompoms use simple sewing or embroidery techniques to make something extra special. All the sewing techniques are easy to learn and do.

Threading a needle

Thread your needle with about 25 in. (65 cm) of thread or yarn (wool). Pull about 6 in. (15 cm) of the thread through the needle. Tie two knots on top of each other at the other end.

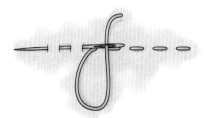

Running stitch

This makes a neat stitch when you are sewing two layers of fabric together.

Secure the end of the thread with a few small stitches. Push the needle down through the fabric a little way along, then bring it back up through the fabric the same distance along. Repeat to form a row of equal stitches.

Backstitch

This is a very useful stitch, since it is strong and similar to the stitches made on a sewing machine. It makes a solid line of stitches.

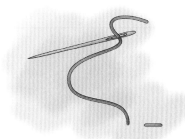

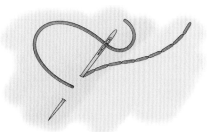

1 Starts as if you were sewing running stitch. Sew one stitch and bring the needle back up to start the second stitch, bringing it up one stitch length ahead.

2 This time, instead of going forward, go back and push the needle through at the end of your first stitch.

3 Bring the needle out again a stitch length ahead. Keep going forward and back to make an even line of stitches with no gaps.

French knot

French knots are useful for sewing tiny eyes and the centers of flowers. They are a bit tricky, so practice on some scrap material first.

Knot your thread and bring the needle up from the back of the fabric to the front. Wrap the thread once or twice around the tip of the needle, then push the needle back in, right next to the place it came up.

As you push the needle in with one hand, hold the wrapped-around threads tightly against the fabric with the thumbnail of your other hand. Pull the needle all the way through. The wraps will form a knot on the surface of the fabric.

Daisy stitch

This uses chain stitch to make a flower shape.

Knot the thread and bring the needle up from the back of the fabric in the center of the flower. Push it back down right beside the place it came up, and bring the needle out again on the edge of the flower shape, looping the thread under the needle tip. Pull the thread through, then take the needle down outside the loop to secure the thread with a tiny stitch. Keep going to sew a group of six to eight single chain stitches in a circle to form a flower shape.

Over stitch or whipstitch

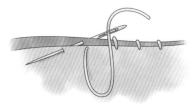

This stitch is used to sew two layers of fabric together with stitches that show at the edges.

Begin with a knot or a few small stitches at the back of the two layers. Push the needle through both layers to the front, a fraction of an inch (2–3 mm) from the edge, and pull the thread right through. Take the needle over the top of both layers to the back again and push it through to the front a little way along the seam. The stitches go over and over the edges of the two fabrics. Finish with a knot or a few small stitches.

Finishing stitching

It is important to finish off all your stitching so that it doesn't come undone. When you have finished stitching, sew a few tiny stitches over and over in the same place on the back of the fabric. Then trim off your thread.

chapter 1

Pompom Creatures

Incy Wincy Spiders

Make your own hairy spiders with popsicle stick webs. Use fun, bright colors for friendly spiders, but use spooky black and orange when it comes to Halloween.

You will need

Popsicle (lolly) craft sticks: 3 red, 3 orange, 3 purple

White (PVA) craft glue

Yarn in cream, lime green, turquoise, and red

Small pompom maker

Pipe cleaners: 2 purple, 2 lime green, 2 turquoise

Pony beads: 8 orange, 8 red, 8 yellow

Googly eyes in different colors

Craft foam in green, purple, and yellow

Scissors

Pencil

1 Start by making the web. Glue three popsicle sticks together in the center, fanning them out equally to make a star shape.

2 Take the cream yarn and hold the end in the center, at the back of the popsicle shape. Take the yarn to the front, take it over the top of the first stick, wrap it around the back, and then on over the top of the next stick. Wrap it around the back again and take it on to the next stick. Keep going around the six spokes of the web.

3 Keep winding around the sticks about eight times more, then turn the web over so the straight lines are at the front. Cut the yarn and glue down the ends.

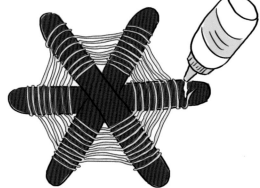

Incy Wincy SPIDER climbed up the spout

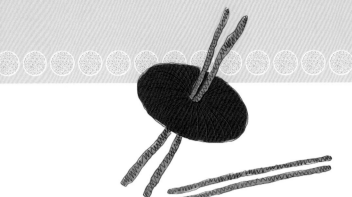

4 To make the spider, wind a small pompom with the red yarn. Before you cut it, cut two turquoise pipe cleaners in half so you have four pieces. Thread them through the center of the pompom ring for the legs. Now cut and tie the pompom off tightly around the legs and remove the rings. Trim and fluff up the pompom and bend the legs into shape.

5 Thread a yellow bead onto the end of each leg and fold the end of the pipe cleaner over to hold it in place.

6 Glue the googly eyes in place. Cut out a small smile shape from foam and stick it on the face. Stick your spider onto its web and let it dry.

7 Use the photographs above and on the previous page as a guide to make spiders in other colors.

Fluffy Kittens

These little pompom kittens are almost as cute as the real thing. Your kitten may be any color you choose and you can have as many as you like in your litter.

1 Make one medium and one small pompom (see page 9). Remove the pompoms, leaving long ties, and fluff up the shape, trimming any uneven strands.

You will need

Small and medium pompom makers

Blunt yarn needle

Scissors

Gray yarn (or your chosen color)

Black yarn, for whiskers

White (PVA) glue

Small piece of gray felt

3D fabric pen

Tip

To add a marmalade kitten to your litter, wrap stripes of orange and yellow yarn around the rings, following the pattern in step 1 of the Buzzy Bee project on page 34.

2 Tie the pompoms together using the long yarn ends (see page 15), so that the smaller pompom becomes the head on top of the body. Trim the ends level with the pompom.

3 Cut four pieces of black yarn, about 4 in. (10 cm) long. Hold the bundle together and tie a knot in the center to make the whiskers. Trim the ends so that they are equal on either side of the knot. Put a dab of glue on the knot and stick to the lower part of the head.

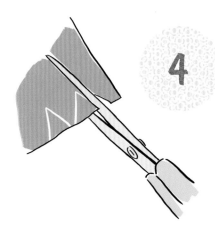

4 Cut two identical triangles from a piece of gray felt—you could make a template from card first so that each ear is the same shape.

5 Glue the ears to the top of the head with a blob of glue. Press in place with your fingers to join the felt to the yarn. Use the 3D fabric pen to add two dots for eyes.

6 Finish your kitty with a long tail. Cut a length of gray yarn and thread it onto the yarn needle. Pass the needle through the center of the larger pompom a few times to secure it in place, then remove the needle, leaving the thread ends attached. Trim one end of the yarn level with the body, and leave the other end long for the tail. Now make some more!

Super cute and SOOO FLUFFY!

Bouncin' Bats

Get ready for trick or treating with these barmy bouncin' bats! Add colorful foam wings and pointy fangs to your pompoms for a truly crazy effect!

You will need

Templates on page 126

Yarn in orange, purple, or lime green

Medium pompom maker

Silver elastic cord

Craft foam in bright colors

Self-adhesive foam in black and white

Scissors

White (PVA) craft glue

Googly eyes

1 Make a medium pompom but instead of tying a piece of yarn around the center, tie a 12-in. (30-cm) piece of silver elastic cord around it, pulling tightly before knotting. Cut and neaten the pompom as normal, leaving the long elastic ends.

2 Copy the templates on page 126 and cut out a pair of wings from the bright craft foam. Cut out two black vein shapes from the self-adhesive black foam and stick to the wings.

boing...boing...BOING!

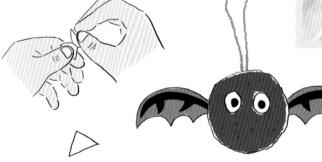

3 Add glue to the inner tip of one of the wings and push it into the pompom to stick it in place. Hold it while it dries. Repeat with the other wing on the opposite side of the pompom.

4 Using the template on page 126, cut out two triangles from the self-adhesive white foam. Stick these fangs to the front of the pompom along with the googly eyes to complete your scary bat!

5 Make more bats using different combinations of yarn and wing colors, then tie the elastic ends together to hang the bats—pull them gently and they will bounce and "fly!"

Bunny in a Hutch

Create this adorable pompom bunny rabbit, then craft a little card hutch for him or her to live in, with a layer of fluffy bedding to make it cozy and warm.

Bunny

You will need

Templates on pages 120–122

Yarn in brown, fluffy cream, and yellow

Small, medium, and large pompom makers

Yarn needle

Tracing paper

Pencil, scissors, and ruler

Felt in pink and gray

White (PVA) craft glue

2 blue wooden beads

Small pink craft pompom

4 pieces of pink cord, 4 in. (10 cm) long

Patterned card

Craft knife (optional)

1 Make one large brown pompom, one medium brown pompom, and one small fluffy cream pompom, leaving the tying ends long. Tie the small cream pompom—the tail—to the large pompom. Take one of the tying ends you have just used in the large pompom and thread this onto a needle. Push it through the center of the large pompom so that it comes out on the opposite side ready to tie to the head. Do the same with the other tying end, then tie the medium brown pompom to the large pompom to make the bunny's head.

2 Copy the ear templates on page 120 and cut out two large ear pieces from gray felt and two small ear pieces from pink felt. Glue the pink centers onto the gray ears and let them dry.

3 Stick the ears, bead eyes, and craft pompom nose in place on the medium pompom to create the face. Push the cord whiskers into the pompom and hold in place until dry.

As **CUTE** as can be!

Hutch

1 To make the hutch, trace the templates on pages 120–122 and transfer them to the patterned card. Be careful to mark on the slots and the door lines accurately. Cut out all the pieces. Insert the tip of your scissors and then cut along the lines for the doors. Use a ruler and the tip of your scissors to score (this means to mark a line with your scissors but not cut all the way through) along the dashed lines on the templates and gently fold the doors open.

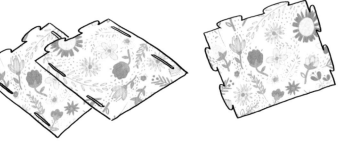

2 Cut out the slots by inserting the point of your scissors into one end and then cutting carefully along it. (You may find it easier to ask an adult to help you cut them with a craft knife.) Insert the flaps on the front piece into the slots on the side pieces. Now do the same with the back piece. Complete by placing the roof on the top of the hutch, carefully pushing the top flaps through the slits.

3 For the hay, make three small pompoms with yellow yarn and place them inside the hutch. Now add your bunny!

Pompom Owl

A family of these cute fluffy owl babies in different colors will look wonderful sitting on a shelf or windowsill. The faces are made using a clever wrapping technique and you will need to make them using a ring pompom maker.

1 Wrap black yarn around the small pompom maker a few times in one place, then cut the yarn and knot it tightly, trimming the ends close. Do the same a finger width away. These make the eyes.

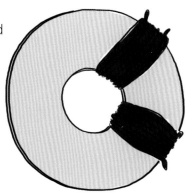

You will need

Template on page 122

Small and medium pompom makers

Yarn in purple, pale pink, cream, black, turquoise, lime green, dark yellow, lemon yellow

Pencil and scissors

Felt in yellow, green, pink, and turquoise

White (PVA) craft glue

Variation

If you'd like to make your owl look realistic, choose a tweedy yarn for the head and body, with flecks of browns, creams, and grays, and use a fluffy yarn for the face.

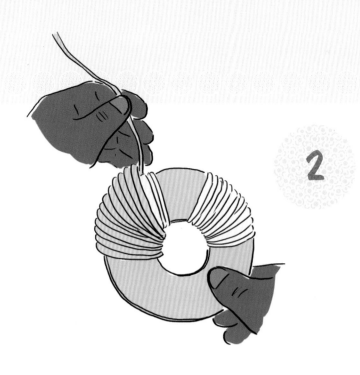

2 Now wrap a layer of cream yarn over both black eyes to cover them completely. Next, cover both the cream sections and the space between them with a continuous wrap of pale pink yarn.

3 Fill the other half of the ring with purple yarn and then wrap one thin layer of purple over the pale pink yarn. Finish the pompom with long ties and remove the card rings. The face will be revealed!

4 Using scissors, trim the face carefully so that more of the purple is revealed, shaping the pale pink into a heart shape.

5 Make a medium purple pompom. Do not cut the central ties but use them to tie the two pompoms together, to join the head to the body (see page 15).

6 Copy the wing template on page 122 and cut out two yellow wings from the felt. Cut a small triangle of green felt for the beak. Glue in place and let them dry completely before releasing into the wild!

7 To make the owls in the other colors, always start with the black and cream for the eyes and then use the photographs as a guide for the other color combinations.

To-wit to-WHOO!

Buzzy Bee

You'll be busy as a bee making this pompom character! Create the yellow and black stripes of the bee by wrapping the yarn in stripes around your pompom maker To display your bee, hang it from a window or ceiling with invisible thread to float in the breeze.

You will need

Black and yellow yarn

Small and medium pompom makers

Scissors

Googly eyes

Mini yellow craft pompom

Scrap of pink felt

White (PVA) craft glue

Silver pipe cleaner

2 black beads with wide center holes

Plate, 7 in. (18 cm) diameter

Yellow tulle fabric

Invisible thread (optional)

 To make the stripy body use the medium pompom maker. Wind the wool neatly in black and yellow stripes around the circle. When you tie it off, leave the ends of the tying yarn long. Release the pompom and fluff up.

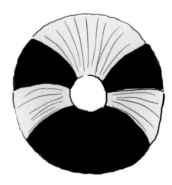

2 For the head, make a small black pompom, again leaving the tails of the tying yarn long. Use the tails to tie the head to the body (see page 15). Glue the googly eyes in place and add a mini yellow craft pompom for the nose. Cut out a pink felt mouth and glue it in place.

3 Cut a piece of pipe cleaner 5 in. (12.5 cm) long. Thread a black bead onto one end, fold the end over and twist it back around the pipe cleaner to hold the bead in place. Do the same on the other end, fold in half, and glue the antennae to the top of the bee's head.

4 Find a plate that is about 7 in. (18 cm) diameter and draw around it on the tulle net. Cut it out and tie a knot in the middle to make the wings. Glue the wings to the back of the stripy pompom.

5 To make a small bee, use the small pompom maker for the body and a mini fork-made pompom for the head. If you want to hang your bees, thread them onto invisible thread.

BEE happy!

Funny Face Hand Puppets

Turn your hand into a monster with these silly puppets. Made with ready-made pompoms and foam from the craft store, they are a quick and easy—great for a puppet show or to make friends laugh.

You will need

Templates on page 120

Large craft pompoms, about 2 in. (5 cm)

Small craft pompoms, about ¾ in. (2 cm)

Mini craft pompoms, about ½ in. (1.5 cm)

Craft foam in assorted colors

Scissors

Large googly eyes

White (PVA) craft glue

Pipe cleaners in assorted colors

Sequins

Variations

Follow the photographs for ideas on all the different styles and combinations, and use the templates as a starting point for your own creations.

1 Using the template on page 120, cut out two foam shapes— we used stars—and stick one to each of the large craft pompoms. Stick the googly eyes on top of these.

2 Take a pipe cleaner and cut it into two lengths, about 6 in. (15 cm) long. Bend into a zigzag shape and glue into the top of the pompom to create an eyebrow. Repeat on the other eye.

3 Alternatively, glue a small pompom to the end of the pipe cleaner and curl the end to make antennae, or decorate the eye with pompoms, or use the templates on page 120 to make eyebrows or eyelashes.

4 Take another pipe cleaner in a different color and trim it to about 10 in. (25 cm). Glue around one end and push well into the pompom underneath the eye. Do the same with the other end and let them dry completely, holding them while they dry.

5 Bend the pipe cleaner into a "W" shape, so you can hold it in your hand easily.

BEND it, SHAPE it, WIGGLE it!

Tulle Birdies

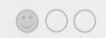

These crazy tulle fabric pompom birds look fab and will add a splash of color to your room dangling over your bed, flying at the window, or suspended from your desk light!

You will need

Template on page 120

Strips of tulle net in bright colors

Large pompom maker

Ribbon

Colored pipe cleaners

Selection of colored beads

Small craft pompoms

Craft foam in white, purple, pink, and orange

White (PVA) craft glue

Scissors

Black pen

1 Cut the tulle into strips about 8 in. (20 cm) long and ¾ in. (2 cm) wide. Using the large pompom maker, wrap the tulle net around it as you would when making a yarn pompom. Cut a piece of colored ribbon about 12 in. (30 cm) long, and tie it around the pompom to finish. Trim the pompom into a ball and knot the ends of the ribbon to make a hanging loop.

2 Thread a brightly colored pipe cleaner through the central tying ribbon. Bend the pipe cleaner in the center and thread beads onto both pieces to create legs, leaving about 1½ in. (4 cm) at the ends. Bend the ends of the pipe cleaner back over to create feet.

3 Glue two craft pompoms onto the face. Cut out two small circles for eyeballs from the white foam (use a small lid or button to draw around), and stick them to the pompoms, then draw a black dot on each one with black pen.

4 Copy the template on page 120 and cut out the beak shape from colored foam. Fold it in half and add a strip of glue along the inside near the fold to keep it half closed. Hold it in place until it dries.

5 Glue around the fold on the top and bottom of the beak and push it between the pompom layers, below the eyes, to complete your crazy bird.

Tweet tweet!

Dippy Dinos

They may look spiky but these are furry, friendly dinosaurs and perfect for snuggling. Choose your favorite dino and recreate it in yarn—we've made a triceratops, stegosaurus, and diplodocus but a T-Rex would be awesome, too!

You will need

Templates on page 123

Yarn in blue, orange, red, purple, turquoise, and yellow

Large, medium, and small pompom makers

Yarn needle

Large metal fork

Craft pompoms in a selection of sizes and colors

Googly eyes

Craft foam in a selection of colors

Pipe cleaners

White (PVA) craft glue

Scissors

Tip

To give your dinosaur a long neck, use a pipe cleaner threaded through the pompoms—see Step 1 of the diplodocus on page 43 for instructions.

Blue stegosaurus

 **1** Make two large pompoms in blue yarn, leaving long tying ends. Use these to tie the two pompoms together to create a very large oval pompom for the body (see page 15). Do not trim the tying ends.

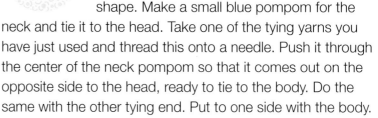

 **2** For the head, make one large pompom with the blue yarn and trim it into an oval shape. Make a small blue pompom for the neck and tie it to the head. Take one of the tying yarns you have just used and thread this onto a needle. Push it through the center of the neck pompom so that it comes out on the opposite side to the head, ready to tie to the body. Do the same with the other tying end. Put to one side with the body.

 3 To make the legs, make four small blue pompoms and tie these to the body using the four long central yarns that you used to tie the body together in step 1. Do not cut the yarns after tying the knots but use them to tie on the neck and head.

4 For the tail, make two small blue pompoms and one red one using the fork technique (see page 12. Tie the blue pompoms together but don't cut the yarns. With the needle, thread the tying ends through the center of one blue pompom so that they come out on the side and use them to tie on the orange pompom, so that you have three pompoms in a line for the tail.

5 Again, thread the needle with one of the tying yarns from the outer blue tail pompom and push it through the center so it comes out on the opposite side ready to tie onto the body To join the tail to the body, use one of the body tying yarns (which you have already used to tie on the legs) thread it onto the needle and push it through the center of the body to the correct position for the tail. Tie on the tail. Trim off all the long tying tarns.

6 For the toes, glue one small and two tiny orange craft pompoms to each leg with the bigger one in the middle. On the face, glue two small green pompoms for the nose and two larger purple pompoms for the eyes. Stick googly eyes on top.

7 Copy the scales templates on page 123 and cut out four small, two medium, and three large scales from green foam. Glue around their bases and push them into the pompoms along the dinosaur's back to make a spine.

Is your **DINO** cute or scary?

Orange triceratops

 1 Make the body and legs as before using orange yarn. For the head, make a large green pompom and trim it into an oval shape, then attach to the body (you do not need a neck in this design). Make the tail with two small orange pompoms and one green fork pompom. Attach to the body.

2 Add the feet as above using green craft pompoms. For the face, use the templates on page 123 to cut out three purple foam horns, a purple foam collar, and the yellow foam veins. Stick the veins to the collar and then glue it around the neck with the horns. Add the eyes as step 6, opposite, to finish.

Purple diplodocus

1 Make the body and legs as before using purple and turquoise yarn wrapped together. Make a head from one large pompom and three fork pompoms and attach to the body. If you would like to give your dino a tall neck, thread a pipe cleaner through the central threads of all the head and neck pompoms to join them together. Add a dab of glue on the end to hold it in place.

2 For the tail, make one small and three fork pompoms, join them together, and attach to the body. Add the feet, nose, and eyes as before.

chapter 2
Celebrate

Pumpkin Wall Hanging

Pumpkins are lumpy and bumpy and come in all shapes and sizes. You need a real one to make a lantern, but this large 3-D wall hanging will look wonderful at a Halloween party or harvest festival celebration.

You will need

Templates on page 126

Pencil and scissors

Orange and green craft foam

Green pipe cleaner

White (PVA) craft glue

Yarn in dark orange, light orange, mustard, and yellow

Large, medium, and small pompom makers

Craft pompoms in red, yellow, and orange

Hole punch

Ribbon, 20 in. (50 cm) long

1 Copy the templates on page 126 and cut out the pumpkin shape from the orange foam. Cut out a stalk shape from the green foam.

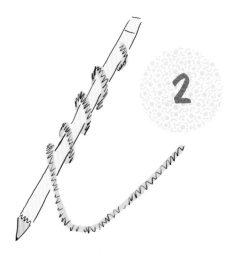

2 Fold the pipe cleaner in half and wrap each half around a pen or pencil to make tendrils.

3 Stick the pipe cleaner and stalk to the main pumpkin piece using craft glue. Let the glue dry completely.

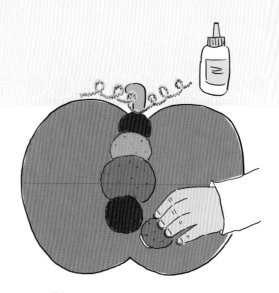

4 Using different color yarns, make three large pompoms, six medium pompoms, and six small pompoms. Trim all the ends.

5 Starting in the center of the pumpkin, arrange the pompoms in a line, with the largest pompom in the middle, then a medium pompom on either side, and two small ones on the ends. Glue them in place with craft glue.

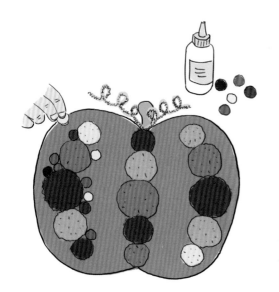

6 Do the same to add two more lines of pompoms on the outer edges, gently curving the lines to follow the shape of the pumpkin. Glue small craft pompoms in between the yarn pompoms to complete the pumpkin.

7 To add a ribbon hanging loop, use one end of a hole punch to make two holes on the top edge of the pumpkin. Thread one end of the ribbon through to the back and tie a large knot, then do the same on the opposite side.

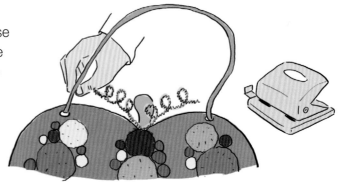

Ghost Garland

When Halloween comes, create a spooky garland with fluffy floating ghosts bobbing along it. Raid your craft stash to add foam mouths and mini pompom eyes to complete your ghastly ghouls.

1 Make a large pompom using the fluffy white yarn, leaving the tying ends long. Rather than trimming the pompom into a round shape, hold the pompom by the long hanging threads and trim the top into a small rounded shape for the head, but leave the bottom full.

You will need

Fluffy white yarn

Large pompom maker

Black self-adhesive foam

Mini craft pompoms—6 black, 6 purple, 6 green

White (PVA) craft glue

Gray yarn

Pen or pencil

Scissors

2 Cut out an oval mouth shape from the self-adhesive black foam, peel off the backing, and stick it to the lower part of the head. Then glue on two of the mini pompoms to make the eyes.

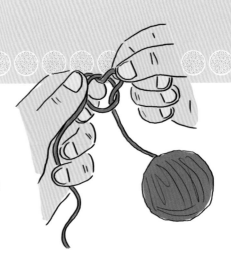

3
For the garland cord, make a length of finger knitting. Take the gray yarn and tie a slip knot. To do this, make a loop in the yarn and hold it with your finger and thumb. With the yarn from the ball behind the loop, pull the yarn through the loop, then pull the loose short end to tighten the knot.

4
Thread the loop onto the index finger of the hand you don't write with, so on your left hand if you are right-handed. With the yarn ends hanging down, take the long end attached to the ball and wrap it over your finger, so it is in front of the loop near the tip of your finger. Now you have two strands of yarn over your finger.

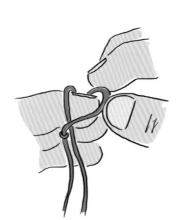

5
Lift the back loop and pull it over the front one and then off your finger. Pull the two ends gently to close the loop and create a "stitch." Repeat until your cord is about 1 yd (1 m) long.

6
To attach the ghost, tie a knot in the hanging threads, 1 in. (2.5 cm) from the pompom. Then tie the ghost to the gray cord. The first knot means that the ghosts will all hang at the same distance from the cord.

7 Repeat steps 1–6 to make six ghosts in total, putting purple and green eyes on the ghosts to add a dash of color. Attach the ghosts at equal distances apart.

WHOOOOOO!!!

Festive Decorations

Christmas is the perfect time to make pompoms that you can turn into decorations. Make this fluffy little Santa and cute robin to hang on the tree below the Angel on page 62. You're sure to think of lots more ideas— try a snowman, penguin, elf, and fairy.

You will need

Small and medium pompom makers

Red, white, and brown yarn

Round object, about 4 in. (10 cm) diameter

Pencil and scissors

Scraps of red, black, and brown felt

White (PVA) craft glue

White mini craft pompom

Black 3-D fabric pen

Brown pipe cleaner

Santa

 1 For the Santa decoration, make one medium pompom from red yarn for the body. Make a small pompom for the head by winding red yarn around the bottom half of the pompom rings and white yarn around the top half. Leave long tying ends for joining the pompoms. Fluff up the pompoms.

 2 Use the long ends to tie the head and body together (see page 15). To make the hat, draw around a round object with a diameter of about 4 in. (10 cm) on a piece of red felt. Fold the felt in half and half again so that you can see the crease lines, and then cut out a quarter circle. Glue the edges of the quarter circle together to make long, thin cone. Glue a mini pompom to the end.

3 Cut a strip of black felt for the belt and glue around the base of the body. Glue the hat to the head and then use a black 3-D fabric pen to add eyes and buttons.

Ho Ho Ho!

Robin

1 For the robin decoration, make a small pompom using brown yarn and then a medium pompom with brown yarn wrapped around half the rings and red yarn around the other half (see step 1, opposite). Tie the pompoms together (see page 15).

2 Cut a tiny triangle from red felt and glue it to the head for a beak. Cut two short pieces of pipe cleaner and wrap them around the ends of a single piece to make the spiky feet. Fold the pipe cleaner in half and glue it into the middle of the body pompom.

Angel Tree Topper

Pop a fluffy pompom angel on the top of your tree or make several angels and line them up on the table or a windowsill for a cute, sparkly festive display.

You will need

10 in. (25 cm) diameter plate or round object

Silver card

Pencil, scissors, and ruler

White (PVA) craft glue

Silver glitter

Stapler

Silver pipe cleaner

White yarn

Small pompom maker

Blue and pink 3-D fabric pens, for the face

Gold pipe cleaner

1 Place the plate on the silver card and draw around it. Draw a line across the center and cut it in half to make a semicircle for the cone.

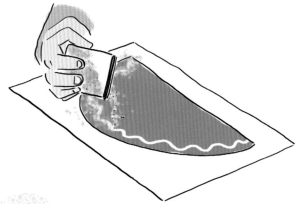

Variations

Use red card to make a Santa tree topper complete with a cotton-ball beard, or a Rudolf the reindeer tree topper using brown card and a pair of antlers!

2 Squeeze a wiggly line of craft glue all around the curved edge of the semicircular piece of card. Sprinkle silver glitter over the glue and leave for a few minutes. Shake off any excess glitter onto a sheet of paper and pour it back into the pot. Let the glue dry completely.

3 Bend the card semicircle into a cone shape and use a stapler to join the card together.

4 Use the whole length of a silver pipe cleaner to form the wings. Twist the ends over to form a figure eight. Apply a dab of glue to the center of the wings and glue them to the back of the cone, about 1¼ in. (3 cm) down from the top. Allow the glue to dry completely.

5 Make a small pompom using white yarn. Spread glue around the point of the cone and push it up into the middle of the pompom to attach it. Let it dry. Use 3-D fabric pens in pink and blue to draw the angel's mouth and eyes on the pompom. Let it dry.

6 For a halo, bend a gold pipe cleaner into a circle with a diameter of about 1¼ in. (3 cm). Twist the ends together, and glue it to the top of the pompom head to finish.

Pompom Tree Decorations

These soft decorations in pale colors will look very sophisticated hanging on your Christmas tree. They are made from embroidered felt shapes threaded with different combinations of pompoms and felt balls.

1 Make four mini pompoms from cream yarn using the fork method (see page 12) and one large pompom, about 4 in. (10 cm) diameter.

2 Draw around a round object with a diameter of about 2½ in. (6 cm) on the felt, and cut out 2 circles. Using embroidery floss, embroider a French knot (see page 17) in the center of one felt circle, then make daisy stitches (see page 17) around the edge to make a flower.

You will need

....

Cream yarn

Large metal fork

Large pompom maker

Round object, about 2½ in. (6 cm) diameter, such as a cup or jar lid

Pencil and scissors

Scraps of felt

Cream embroidery floss (thread)

Embroidery needle

Small and large felt balls in matching or contrasting colors (or make your own, see page 106)

Sewing needle and matching thread

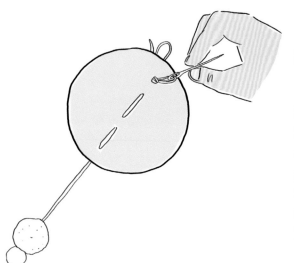

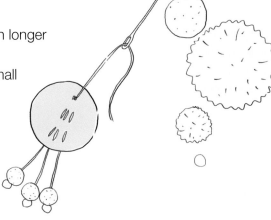

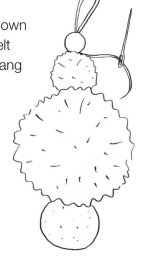

3 To attach the hanging pompoms, take a length of cream floss, thread it on a large needle, and make a knot in the end. Pass the needle through a small felt ball and then through the center of a mini pompom. Make a couple of small stitches (without going all the way through the felt) in the undecorated felt circle, pull through the thread to get the balls hanging at the right level, and then secure the thread with a couple of small stitches over and over in the same place. Cut the thread. Do the same for one more hanging bauble.

4 For the last hanging bauble use a much longer length of floss. Start in the same way, securing the thread with a couple of small stitches in the felt, but don't cut the thread. Instead, take the needle out through the top of the felt and thread on a small felt ball, a large felt ball, the large pompom, a mini pompom, and a small felt ball.

Tip

Felt balls are available at craft supply stores and online but you can make your own—see page 106 for how to make a felted ball.

5 Take the needle back down through the top small felt ball, leaving a loop to hang the decoration. Secure the thread by making a few stitches through the felt ball.

6 Place the embroidered circle shape on the back circle shape with wrong sides facing (so the embroidery is on the outside). Sew the felt circles together with small over stitches (see page 17) all around the edge.

How many pompoms can you thread on?

Snowball Decorations

These supersoft snowballs are made from T-shirt fabric. You can use almost any material to make a pompom, and this is a great way of recycling old clothes. Hang the snowballs with baker's twine, or simply have a pretend snowball fight!

You will need

Template on page 124

Cardboard

Scissors

Pen and ruler

Fabric scissors

White T-shirt or tank top

1 yd (1 m) baker's twine, string, or yarn

White (PVA) craft glue

Iridescent white glitter

2 bowls or plates

 1 Lay the T-shirt out on a table and smooth it flat. Measure along both side seams from the bottom and mark every ¾ in. (2 cm). Cut off the thick hem at the bottom and then cut the T-shirt into strips, using your marks as a guide—it doesn't matter if the strips are not completely straight or an even width.

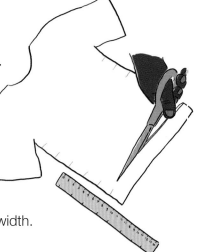

2 The strips will be in loops, so snip along the seam on one side of each strip to make them into long lengths.

3 Cut out two card rings using the template on page 9. Cut out a small section through the side to make it easier to wind the fabric. Wind your T-shirt strips around the rings just like you would with yarn, but going backward and forward from one side of the slit to the other, until you have covered it with three or four layers of fabric.

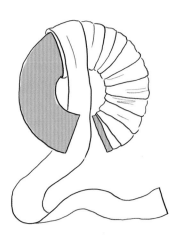

4 Cut through the layers of fabric, between the two rings. Wrap the baker's twine between the rings and tie it tightly. Remove the rings and fluff up the pompom. Tie the ends of the baker's twine together to make a loop for hanging.

5 Pour craft glue into one bowl and glitter into another. Dip the pompom into the glue and keep turning it until the glue coats the ends of the fabric all round. Now dip it into the glitter, and turn it until the pompom is covered in glitter. Shake off the excess, and let the glue dry before hanging your snowball decoration.

Variation

Use a larger ring and colored fabric strips to make cheerleader pompoms instead. For more cheerleading ideas, see page 98.

Soft and SPARKLY!

Pompom Angels

We've made these sweet little angels, with their delicate paper-doily wings and golden haloes, in soft pastel colors, but you can use any color yarn to make a pretty Christmas decoration for the tree or festive table.

You will need

Medium and large pompom makers

Scissors

Pale pink, blue, or white yarn

White (PVA) craft glue

Small paper doily

3 small pearl beads for the angel's eyes and mouth

Gold pipe cleaner for the halo

Invisible thread (optional)

1 Make a medium and large pompom in your chosen yarn color, leaving the tying ends long. Use the long yarn ends to tie the two pompoms together (see page 15), then trim the ends.

2 Fold the paper doily in half, crease it, and cut along the crease with scissors to make two semicircles. Fold each semicircle in half again to make a triangular wing, and then glue the points of the wings to the center back of the larger pompom.

3 Use dots of glue to stick the pearl eyes and mouth to the front of the smaller pompom, which forms the angel's head.

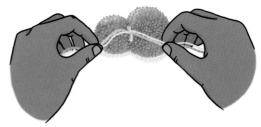

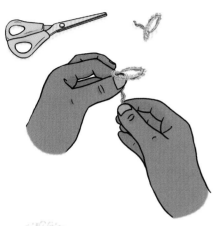

4 To make the halo, form a circular shape, about 1 in. (2.5 cm) in diameter, with the gold pipe cleaner. Twist the ends to secure them in place and trim them with scissors.

5 Stick the halo to the top of the angel's head with glue. To hang your angel, attach a length of yarn or invisible thread around the neck and tie to make a hanging loop.

ANGELIC additions to the tree

Clothes Pin Fairy

This sweet fairy is a traditional figure in parts of Europe and South America, where she brings Christmas gifts. We've used multicolored, rainbow yarn for her skirt, but use any to fit your color scheme. She carries her gifts in a gold painted matchbox.

You will need

Template on page 124

Thin card (a cereal packet works well)

Pencil and scissors

Wooden clothes pin

Small matchbox, about 2 x 1¼ in. (5 x 3.5 cm)

Gold acrylic paint and paintbrush

Black fine tip marker pen

Yellow yarn

White (PVA) craft glue

Large pompom maker

Rainbow yarn

Approx 9 in. (23 cm) florist's wire

16 in. (40 cm) narrow red ribbon

Tip
If your ribbon slips a little, add a dab of glue underneath to hold it in place.

1 Copy the heart template on page 124 draw round it onto thin card, and cut out a small heart for the fairy's wings. Paint the heart, clothes pin, and matchbox with gold acrylic paint and let them dry.

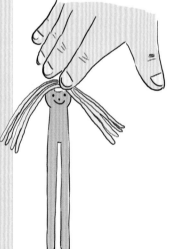

2 Using a black marker pen, draw eyes, a nose, and a mouth onto the clothes pin. Cut four 3-in (8-cm) lengths of yellow yarn. Spread some glue onto the top of the clothes pin head and press on the yarn. You may want to give her a little haircut at this point.

3 Make a large pompom with rainbow yarn. Keep going until you have covered the card with three or four layers of yarn.

A GIFT for the tree

4 The next step is tricky and might be easier if you have two pairs of hands! Cut a 12 in. (30 cm) piece of yarn for tying off the pompom. Then, as for a normal pompom, insert your scissors between the two layers of cardboard and cut around the pompom. This time, before you tie it off, carefully push the clothes pin doll through the center hole and hold her there while you wind the yarn tightly around the pompom and the doll so that she is fixed in the center of the pompom. Remove the card rings and trim the tie.

5 Wind the piece of florist's wire twice around the doll, just above the pompom. Bend the wire arms about 1¼ in. (3 cm) from each end and push them into either end of the matchbox so that she holds it flat. Glue the heart wings to the back, over the wire. To finish, tie the red ribbon around the box in a bow.

Easter Lamb Mobile

Celebrate the arrival of spring with this Easter lamb mobile. Made from fluffy wool, the lambs look as if they are jumping through the fields. It would be a perfect gift to hang over the crib of a new baby.

1 Make two large fluffy white pompoms and tie them together using the central tying threads to make an even larger oval pompom (see page 15). Don't trim the tying threads. Make a small black pompom using the fork technique (see page 12). Don't trim the tying threads. Thread the needle onto one of the white tying threads and push it through the center of one of the white pompoms to the correct position to tie on the head. Tie on the black pompom. Trim to neaten.

2 Cut a pipe cleaner in half, bend it in the middle to make a pair of legs, and then fold the ends to make feet. Do the same with the other half of pipe cleaner. Glue along the bend of the pipe cleaner legs and push them into the pompom underneath the body, holding in place until the glue dries.

You will need

Templates on pages 124–125

Fluffy white yarn

Large pompom maker

Black yarn

Large metal fork

Yarn needle

3 black pipe cleaners

Scissors

White (PVA) craft glue

6 googly eyes

Small white craft pompoms

Large sheet of medium weight card (A3)

Hole punch

Pale blue paint and paintbrush (latex/emulsion paint works well)

Yellow ribbon

Sheet of thin yellow card (A4)

Paper clips or clothes pins (pegs) (optional)

Sewing thread

Sticky tack

3 Glue two googly eyes to the face and a craft pompom on the bottom for a tail. Make two more lambs following steps 1–3.

4 Copy the hanger templates on page 124 and cut out of the shapes from the medium weight card. Use a hole punch to make the holes marked on the template.

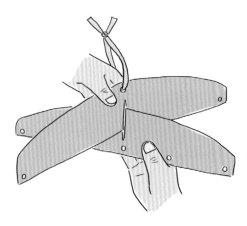

5 Paint the hanger shapes all over with pale blue paint and let them dry. Thread a piece of yellow ribbon about 10 in. (25 cm) long through the top hole and tie in a knot. Place the slotted sections together to create the hanger.

6 Copy the template on page 125 and cut two fence shapes from the yellow card. Take care cutting out the central panels—insert the point of your scissors in the center and cut around the inner edge. Punch out the holes marked on the template.

7 Glue the two fence pieces together to make a long strip and then bend them around to create a ring. Glue the ends in place—use a paper clip or clothes pin (peg) to hold the ends together as they dry.

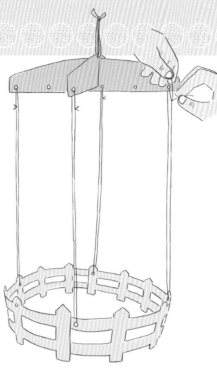

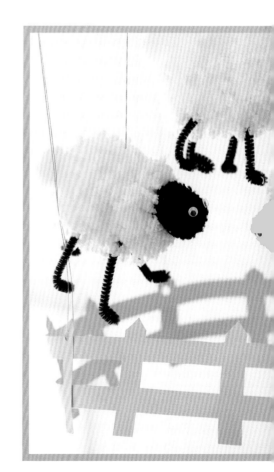

8 Cut four lengths of sewing thread about 23½ in. (60 cm) long. Thread one of these through to join a hole in the fence and then through a hole on the outside arm of the hanger and knot the ends together in a loop using a reef knot (see page 15). Do this to join all the outer hanger holes to the fence. Be careful when you knot the threads that you keep them all the same length so that the fence hangs straight.

9 Cut a length of thread about 16 in. (40 cm) long. Wrap the center around the middle of a lamb and knot it to hold the lamb in place, then tie it to the central hole on the hanger Adjust it so the lamb hangs straight at the bottom. Cut two slightly longer pieces of thread, about 20 in. (50 cm) long, and use these to tie the remaining lambs to the other holes. Hang up your mobile— if it doesn't hang quite straight use small pieces of sticky tack to balance it.

Baaaa! Baaaa! Baaaa!

Speckled Eggs and Chick ☺ ☺ ○

Make a box of speckledy, stripy, and spotty eggs to give as an Easter gift. One has already hatched into a cute, fluffy chick to tuck in alongside them. Wrapping the pastel yarns in different patterns and layers creates these gorgeous effects.

You will need

Template on page 122

Yarn in pretty pastel colors —we used yellow, blue, lilac, coral, peach, lime green, and mint green

Large and medium pompom makers

Fork

Small googly eyes

Pencil and scissors

White (PVA) craft glue

Egg carton

White paint

Paintbrush

Pieces of felt in orange and yellow

Tip

Some of these special effects are easier to make with a plastic pompom maker, which splits into two halves so you don't have to push the yarn through a center hole.

Eggs

 1 To make the striped eggs, choose three colors; we used peach, green, and coral. Wrap the yarn in wide stripes around the large pompom maker.

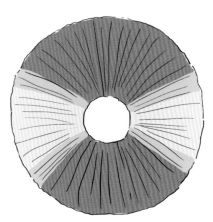

2 Finish the pompom and remove from the rings. Now trim the pompom into an oval egg shape. Use the yellow, lime green, and blue yarn to make the other striped egg.

3 To make the pink marbled egg, hold the lilac, coral, and peach yarns together and wrap them around the large pompom maker so that the colors are mixed together randomly. Finish the egg as in step 2. For the blue/green version, use the lime green, mint green, and blue yarns.

4 For the spotty egg, wrap 12-in. (30-cm) lengths of mint green yarn around small sections of the large pompom maker. Now cover the entire pompom maker with a layer of lilac yarn.

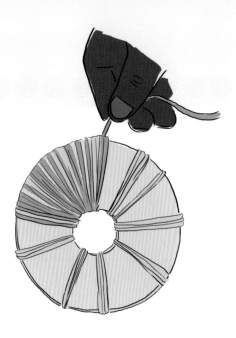

5 Now add another couple of sections of mint yarn. Repeat steps 4 and 5 until the pompom maker is covered thickly. Then shape the egg as in step 2. Make the yellow and blue egg in the same way.

6 Paint an egg carton with white paint, inside and out, and let it dry completely before using it to display the eggs.

Chick

1 Make a medium yellow pompom and a yellow mini fork pompom (see page 12). Leave the tying yarn ends long and use these to tie them together (see page 15). Copy the template on page 122 and cut out two yellow wings and an orange beak from the felt. Stick them onto the chick as shown, along with the googly eyes.

Mini Pompom Cake Toppers

Finish your home-baked cupcakes with these pretty pompoms made from tissue paper and washi tape. The cute decorations look like trendy cake pops, and will look really impressive at any celebration.

1 Fold the sheet of tissue paper in half and then into quarters, then fold again along the shortest side three times into a concertina, until you have a folded strip of paper about 2½ in. (6 cm) wide with 16 layers of tissue.

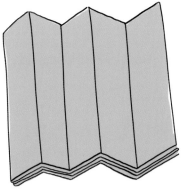

You will need

Makes 8 cake toppers

Template on page 119

2 sheets of tissue paper, 20 x 30 in. (50 x 75 cm)

Paper, pencil, and scissors

Sticky tack

Push pin (drawing pin)

8 mini brads (paper fasteners)

8 wooden skewers or cake pop sticks, 6 in. (15 cm) long

Double-sided foam tape, ½ in. (1 cm) wide

Decorative or colored washi tape (optional)

Tip

To make a larger cake topper, simply fold your tissue paper into a wider strip and use a larger circle for a template.

2 Copy the circle template on page 119. Mark the center with your pencil and then make a hole through it. Place it on the folded tissue paper and draw around it four times. Mark the center of the circle by pushing your pencil through the hole in the template. Repeat with the second piece of tissue paper.

3 Put a piece of sticky tack behind each circle in turn and use a push pin (drawing pin) to push a hole all the way through to the back. Then push (you may need to wiggle and twist) a brad (paper fastener) through the hole and open out the two pins at the back. Carefully cut out the circles to create a stack of tissue circles. The brad will keep the circles together as you cut. You will have four stacks of green and fours stacks of pink.

4 Using the template as a guide, make straight cuts in the circles with the tips of your scissors, cutting from the outside edge in toward the center. Cut as close as you can to the brad. You'll find that the paper shifts as you cut the straight lines, but this is fine as it helps with the feathering effect.

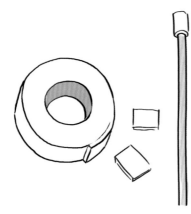

5 Cut a ¾-in. (2-cm) length of double-sided foam tape, peel off the backing tape on one side, and wrap the sticky side around the top of a wooden skewer or cake pop stick. Peel off the second layer of tape backing so it is sticky on the outside.

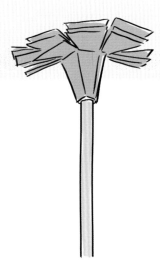

6 Now count up eight layers of your paper stack and push the taped end of the stick between this and the next layer, pushing it right inside toward the brad. Pull down three or four flaps of paper over the top of the stick and gently squeeze them over the tape until the pompom feels securely stuck.

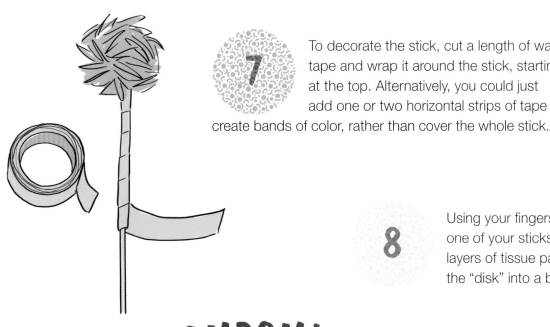

7 To decorate the stick, cut a length of washi tape and wrap it around the stick, starting at the top. Alternatively, you could just add one or two horizontal strips of tape to create bands of color, rather than cover the whole stick.

8 Using your fingers or the end of one of your sticks, separate the layers of tissue paper to fluff up the "disk" into a ball shape.

Pop in a POMPOM!

Pompom Play Food

These strawberries, cupcakes, and ice cream cones look almost good enough to eat! Make a few, then try adapting the designs to make your own tea party menu. You will get plenty of practice in trimming pompoms to shape—it's a bit like cutting hair!

You will need

Template on page 123

Yarn in cream, red, green, beige, pale pink, turquoise, and yellow

Small, medium, and large pompom makers

Scissors

Patterned cupcake cup

Assorted sequins

Red wooden bead

White (PVA) craft glue

Yarn needle

Patterned paper

Double-sided sticky tape

Small red craft pompom

Strawberry

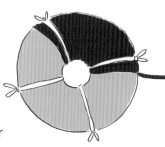

 1 Use a medium cardboard ring pompom maker. Cut four pieces of cream yarn, 8 in. (20 cm) long. Tie the yarn around the pompom maker, spacing them at regular intervals. Wrap a layer of red yarn over the cream threads.

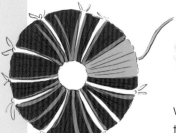

2 Repeat step 1 until your pompom maker is covered thickly, spacing out the cream threads in different places each time and covering with red yarn. Wrap the green yarn about ten times in one place.

3 Cut through the red and cream threads through the pompom rings, but leave the green uncut. Thread through a length of red yarn and tie off the pompom as normal, then remove the card rings (you will have to cut through the cardboard). With the loops of green yarn at the top, trim the red and cream yarn into a heart shape to look like a strawberry, trimming the red yarn around the green loops so that it is quite short.

4 Leave one loop of green yarn in the center and trim the tops off the other green loops until they are about ½ in. (1 cm) long, to make the leaves. Twist the central loop, or knot its base, to make it stand up as the stalk.

Cupcake

 1 Make one large pale pink and one large beige pompom. Do not cut the central yarn threads but use these to tie them together (see page 15). Trim and shape the beige section into a cupcake shape with straight sides and a flat base. Shape the pale pink frosting section into a round, dome shape.

 2 Glue the pompom cupcake into the cupcake cup. Glue on sequin sprinkles and a wooden bead cherry, to decorate.

TEA is served!

Ice cream cone

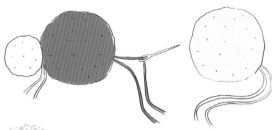

1 Make one large yellow, one large turquoise, and one small cream pompom. Use the tying threads to tie the turquoise pompom to the small cream pompom (see page 15). Then take the needle and thread it with one of the tying yarns you have just used. Push it through the center of the turquoise pompom so that it comes out on the opposite side to the cream pompom. Use it to tie on the large yellow pompom so that the three pompoms are all in a line.

2 Copy the template on page 123 and cut a cone from the patterned paper. Put a strip of double-sided sticky tape on one of the straight sides. Roll into a cone shape, peel off the backing strip, and stick the edges in place.

3 Glue the pompoms inside the cone and complete your ice cream by gluing a small craft pompom cherry on the top.

Pompom Party Hats

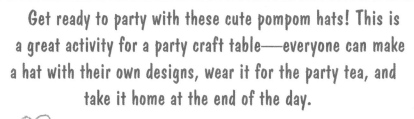

Get ready to party with these cute pompom hats! This is a great activity for a party craft table—everyone can make a hat with their own designs, wear it for the party tea, and take it home at the end of the day.

You will need

Makes 3 hats

Template on page 123

Pencil and scissors

Felt-tipped pens

Large sheets of thin card in yellow, green, and blue

Double-sided tape

Sticky tape

Yarn in different colors—we used yellow, lime green, turquoise, and neon pink

Large pompom maker (a plastic pompom maker tool will speed things up at a party!)

White (PVA) craft glue

Pompom trim in yellow, blue, and green

Ribbon, cut into 18 in. (45 cm) lengths: 2 yellow, 2 blue, 2 green

Craft pompoms, about ¾ in. (2 cm) diameter: 2 yellow, 2 blue, 2 green

1 Using the template on page 123, cut out the hat shape from the colored card. Use the felt-tipped pens to draw patterns on the shape—we used pink zigzags, purple, orange, and turquoise stars, green wavy lines, and yellow dots.

2 Stick a piece of double-sided tape along one straight edge. Peel off the protective strip, roll the shape into a cone, and stick the edge in place. You may want to add a piece of sticky tape over the join for extra strength.

3 Hold the ends of the yarns together and wind them around the large pompom maker using the different balls of yarn at the same time, to quickly create a multicolored ball. If using cardboard rings, cut a section out of the ring to make winding with multiple strands easier.

PARTY fun for everyone

4 Trim and fluff up the pompom. Glue around the point of the hat and push this right into the center of the pompom to hold it in place. Measure around the base of the hat with a piece of pompom trim, cut it to size, and glue it to the rim.

5 To finish the hat with ties, glue a craft pompom to the end of each piece of ribbon, then stick the other end to the inside of the hat, either with glue or a piece of sticky tape—or both for extra strength!

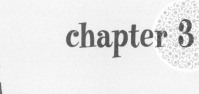

chapter 3

Accessories

Wrapped Bangle

Really tiny pompoms are difficult to make but you can buy them joined together on a trim and they are perfect for these unusual bangles. The bangles are super-quick and easy to make ,so why not make lots in different colors to give as friendship bracelets.

You will need

Green pompom trim

Plastic bangles

Scissors

White (PVA) craft glue

Masking tape (optional)

Pink yarn

Yarn needle

1 Take the pompom trim and wrap it around the bangle. Cut it so it is the same size as the bangle with no overlap. Stick it around the center of the bangle with a line of glue. If it keeps slipping on the wet glue, use some pieces of masking tape to hold it in place until the glue dries.

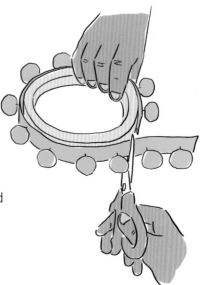

2 Cut a 40-in. (1-m) piece of pink yarn and wind it around your hand to make a ball. Now start wrapping it tightly around the bangle, flattening down the strings of the pompom trim as you work. Be careful not to leave any gaps where you can still see the bangle underneath.

Variation

For the rhinestone bangle, glue a length of rhinestone trim to the center of the bangle, wrap yellow embroidery floss around the bangle between each rhinestone, working in one direction, and then wrap pink floss in the opposite direction, to create a criss-cross effect.

All wrapped up!

Once you get back to the start, tie the two yarn ends into a knot on the inside of the bangle but don't cut the ends. Hide them instead by threading the yarn needle with both the ends of the yarn (if this is too difficult, do one at a time) and pushing the needle through the wraps of yarn inside the bangle. Finally, pull off the needle and trim any of the ends that still show.

Caterpillar Bag Charm

This bright and colorful caterpillar bag charm is sure to brighten up your school bag! The pompom critter is sewn to a felt leaf, on which he is happily munching away!

You will need

Template on page 125

Yarn in pink, turquoise, and yellow

Large metal fork

Thick green felt

Pen and scissors

Green felt-tipped pen

Yarn needle

Needle threader (optional)

Googly eyes

Pink metallic pipe cleaner, cut into 4-in. (10-cm) length

White (PVA) craft glue

Green ribbon

Lobster clasp

Tip
There is quite a lot of threading needles to be done in this project so a needle threader might be useful.

1 Using the fork technique (see page 12), make two pink, two turquoise, and one yellow pompom. Leave long ends of the tying yarn. Tie a pink and yellow pompom together (see page 15), then tie a turquoise and pink pompom together. Do not cut the long yarn ends—you will need them again.

2 Copy the leaf template on page 125, draw around it onto the thick green felt, and cut it out. Draw the veins onto the leaf using a green felt-tipped pen, following the template or making up your own design. Allow to dry.

3 Now sew the caterpillar to the leaf. Take the pink and turquoise pompom pair and thread one long end of pink yarn onto a yarn needle, push the needle through from the front to the back of the leaf near where the bite is and pull the yarn end through. Remove the needle and repeat with the second long pink end. Now do the same with the two turquoise ends. Tie all the ends together in a knot underneath, making sure that the pompoms are pulled tight against the felt on the top. Repeat with the other pair of pompoms and the single turquoise pompom, arranging them in a line to make the caterpillar. Now trim the ends on the back of the leaf.

4 To finish your caterpillar, stick the googly eyes to the head. Thread the pipe cleaner under the second pompom, just behind the stitch through the felt and then twist it together once, between the two pompoms so it can't fall off. Now shape it into a pair of curly antennae and stick it in place against the back of the head with a couple of spots of glue.

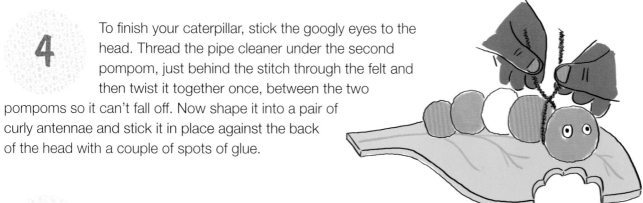

5 Carefully make a hole at the bottom of the leaf with the end of your scissors and thread the ribbon through it, thread the lobster clasp on, and tie a knot in the ribbon to secure.

A very hungry **CATERPILLAR**

Pompom Necklace

Making jewelry with pompoms is a fun activity for a rainy afternoon. You only use small pompoms, so they are quick to make and the whole necklace is very easy to put together—use all your favorite colors and make it as long or short as you like.

You will need

4 balls of yarn in assorted colors

Scissors

Yarn needle

Small pompom maker

1 Cut a length of yarn long enough to make a necklace that will fit over your head easily, and thread your needle on the end. Cut another long length of yarn in your first pompom color and begin winding around the pompom maker.

2 When you have finished winding the pompom, push your prepared needle and yarn through the center, then cut around the edge of the pompom ring with scissors. Keep the needle threaded.

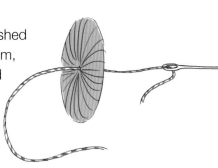

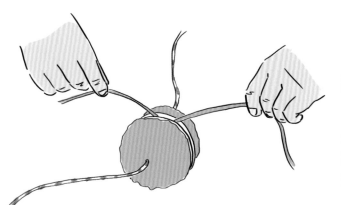

3 Take a short length of yarn that matches the pompom and wrap it between the two halves of the pompom rings. Tie it tightly in a knot and then cut off the extra yarn. Remove the pompom rings to leave the finished pompom in place on the necklace.

FABULOUS, FLUFFY, and FUN

4 Make more pompoms to give a total of about 11 (an odd number works best, with one in the center and an even number on each side). Add them to the necklace in the same way.

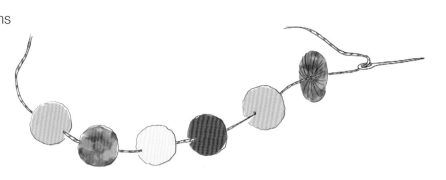

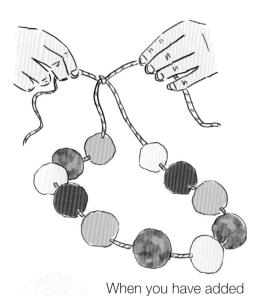

5 When you have added all the pompoms, remove the needle and tie the ends of the necklace yarn together. Check in a mirror to get it the right length. The pompoms will move slightly on the yarn and you can position them so that they are evenly spaced along your necklace.

Poodle Phone Case

Protect your phone with this funky pompom poodle case made from soft felt and yarn. Add a ribbon bow to the poodle's topknot for a super-cute finishing touch worthy of any pampered pooch!

You will need

Templates on page 125

Pencil and scissors

Felt in pink, dark pink, and green

Pins

White (PVA) craft glue

Pink yarn

Large metal fork

Yarn needle

Small googly eyes

Mini black craft pompom

Pink embroidery floss (thread) and needle

1 Copy the templates on page 125 and cut them out. Draw around the ears, tail tip, and body shape on the pink felt, and the head, legs, and tail on the dark pink felt. Cut out all the shapes.

2 Fold the green felt so that it is double and pin it together. Put your phone on top and draw around it, making the shape a little larger all round. Cut around the rectangle so that you have two identical pieces.

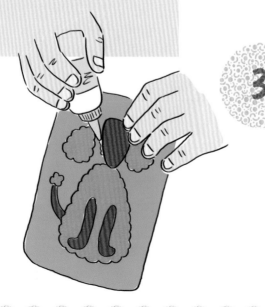

3 Arrange the poodle felt pieces on one of the green rectangles and glue them in place with craft glue, starting with the body and ears.

4 Make four mini pompoms using the fork method (see page 12). Leave the tying threads long and trim the pompoms into a ball shape.

BEST in show!

5 Take one pompom and thread one long end onto a yarn needle. Position the pompom on the end of one leg and push the needle through from the front to the back of the felt, pulling the yarn end through. Remove the needle and repeat with the second long end. Tie the ends together in a knot at the back, making sure that the pompom is pulled tight against the felt on the top. Do the same to add pompoms on the other leg, the chest, and head.

6 Take a piece of stripy pink ribbon and tie a bow (see page 14). Trim the ends neatly and glue the bow to the top of the head pompom. Glue the eyes and mini craft pompom nose in place.

7 Pin the other green rectangle to the back of the poodle. Thread your embroidery needle with a length of floss and knot the end. Starting at the top, bring the needle out from inside the felt case on the edge and sew around the side and bottom edges using over stitch (see page 17).

Pompom Tote Bag

When you have become an expert pompom maker you can use them to decorate all kinds of things, like this fun bag. it uses some sewing skills, with pompoms as the finishing touch.

1 To make the bag, cut a rectangle of fabric 11 x 29 in. (28 x 74 cm). Cut two strips of fabric, 3½ x 18 in. (9 x 45 cm) for the handles. Fold each strip in half lengthwise and pin. Sew along the open edge, about ½ in. (1 cm) in, using backstitch (see page 16), or use a sewing machine.

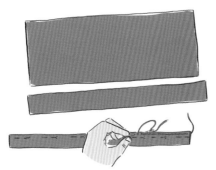

You will need

Felt or fleece fabric, about ½ yd (0.5 m)

Fabric scissors

Pins

Sewing needle and matching thread, or sewing machine

Large safety pin

Knitting needle (optional)

Yarn in 3 different colors

Small pompom maker

White (PVA) craft glue

Felt stars (optional)

Tip
Use a felted or fleece fabric for the bag as the edges won't fray, which makes sewing the seams much easier!

2 Turn the handles right sides out—this can be tricky but try attaching a large safety pin to one end and then pushing the pin back into the tube of fabric. Feed it through until it comes out the other end and then pull through gently. Pushing the fabric with the blunt end of a knitting needle can also help. Use your fingers to press the handle flat, with the seam along the center of the back.

3 Take the rectangle of fabric, fold over both short edges by 1½ in. (4 cm, and pin in place. Sew along the edge of the hems in backstitch or use the sewing machine.

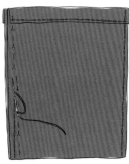

4 Fold the bag in half so that the right sides are facing (hemmed edges on the outside) and pin in place. Backstitch or machine stitch ½ in. (1 cm) in from both side edges. Turn the bag right side out.

5 Pin one handle to the inside of the bag, with the seam facing in. Line the ends up with the edge of the hem and position them about 2¾ in. (7 cm) from the sides. Pin them and then backstitch in place, sewing in a rectangle around the end of the handle. Do the same with the other handle, making sure that they match up.

 **6** Make four pompoms in different colors of yarn, or make them all the same if you like! Sew the pompoms along the top of one side of the bag, spacing them about ½ in. (1 cm) apart and about ¾ in. (2 cm) in from the sides. Thread a needle with a long thread and secure the thread on the inside of the bag. Bring your needle through the bag and then through the center of the pompom and back again, pulling the thread through so the pompom is tight against the bag. Do this a few times and then move on to the next pompom. When you have sewn on all four, secure the thread with a few stitches over and over in one place on the inside of the bag.

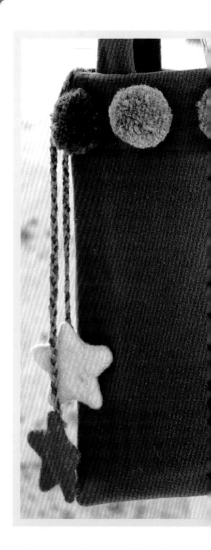

7 If you'd like to add the hanging stars, take six strands of yarn about 16 in. (40 cm) long (two strands of three colors), knot them all together at one end, and attach the knot to a pillow (cushion) with a safety pin, or ask a friend to hold it for you. Separate the yarn into pairs of the same color and braid (plait) the yarn together (see page 14) to make a long tie. Knot the end.

8 Sew a felt star in place at the end of the braid with a few stitches, then sew the other end of the braid to the top of the bag. Repeat to make a second braid.

Pompom Bookmarks

Never lose your place again with these fun and funky pompom bookmarks. Why not make one for a friend, complete with an embroidered initial? You can use the shapes provided in the templates section on page 124, or invent your own.

You will need

Templates on page 124

Pencil and scissors

Yarn in different colors

Large metal fork

Felt in different colors

Embroidery floss (thread) in different colors

Embroidery needle

Pins

1 Using the fork technique (see page 12), wrap the yarn around the tines. Cut three pieces of yarn about 24 in. (60 cm) long, hold them together, and tie the middle of these pieces around the center of the wrapped yarn before removing from the fork. You need to end up with six long ends, all about the same length. Trim the pompom into a fluffy ball.

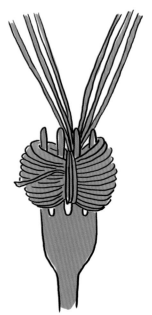

2 Divide the six yarn ends into three sections of two strands each. Braid (plait) the pairs of yarn ends to make a braid 8 in. (20 cm) long (see page 14). Tie a knot and trim the ends to neaten them.

Perfect gifts for BOOKWORMS!

3 Using the templates on page 124, cut out two matching shapes from the felt. If you would like to add an initial, lightly draw a letter on one felt shape in pencil. Thread your needle with embroidery floss in a different color to the felt, and backstitch (see page 16) along the marked shape. When you've finished, secure your thread on the back with a few stitches over and over.

4 Pin the felt shapes together, trapping the knotted end of the braid in between the shapes. Thread the needle with a different color of floss. Secure the thread on the inside of the shapes and bring the needle out on the edge, then sew around the edge using small neat running stitches (see page 16). When you sew across the braid make sure that you catch the braid in your stitches so it can't pull out.

5 To make the star and flower designs, simply repeat steps 1–4, using different combinations of yarn and felt colors, and following the photo as a guide.

Cheerleading Pompoms

Get together with some friends and each make a set of these red, white, and blue tissue paper pompoms. Then create your own cheers and dance routines, just for fun or to cheer on your school teams.

You will need

Large tissue paper sheets:
10 red, 10 white, 10 blue

Ruler and pencil

Large scissors

Sticky tape

Sparkly duct tape (optional)

Tip

You could use normal duct or parcel tape if you can't find the sparkly tape in your local craft store.

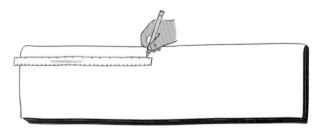

1 Lay the sheets of tissue paper in front of you in three piles—one for each color. Start to make a separate pile using one sheet of each color (red, white, blue), and keep adding sheets in order, until there are 15 sheets in the pile. Fold the pile in half with the long edges together.

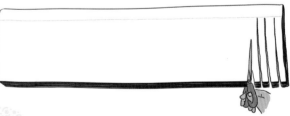

2 Measure in 2 in. (5 cm) from the folded edge in four or five places. Join the marks with a ruler and pencil to make a line parallel to the fold. Starting on the unfolded edge, and working along the whole length, cut ½-in. (1-cm) wide strips, stopping at your marked line. Make sure you do not cut along the folded edge as this holds the pompom together.

3 Neatly roll the paper up along the folded edge and then hold the rolled edge in place using a few pieces of sticky tape. This makes the handle for your pompom.

4 To add a bit of sparkle and make the handle easier to hold, you can wrap some sparkly duct tape around the taped end. Repeat steps 1–4 with the remaining tissue paper to make the second pompom.

GO TEAM!

Bag Charm

This fun accessory will look great on your school bag! It's the perfect project for using up any spare pompoms or scraps of yarn, and you can raid your craft stash to find pretty beads and ribbons to add extra decoration.

You will need

Yarn in different colors

Small pompom maker

Yarn needle

Ribbon

Sticky tape

Wooden beads

Key chain

White (PVA) craft glue

1 Make two or three pompoms in different colors—vibrant, clashing colors will look great. When you tie them around the center, leave long tails of yarn for attaching the pompoms to the keychain later or, if you like, tie a different color yarn around the center of the pompom to add a contrasting color.

2 Cut a length of ribbon, about 5 or 6 in. (12 or 15 cm) long. Tie a knot at one end of the ribbon, then thread on some wooden beads. It is easier to thread the beads if you wrap a piece of sticky tape around the end of the ribbon.

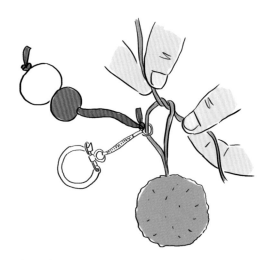

3 Make up two or three ribbons with beads. Tie the ribbons and pompoms to the end of the key chain, knotting the yarn or ribbon tightly, and tying them so they are all different lengths.

4 To keep your charms in place, add a dab of craft glue to the knots. Let the glue dry completely before attaching to your bag.

Totally CHARMING!

chapter 4

Decorate

Paper Pompoms

Brighten up your bedroom with these gorgeous paper pompoms. Make them in different sizes and colors and hang them at different heights where they will blow in the breeze from your window. Quick and easy to make, they'd also be perfect for a party.

You will need

Makes a set of 5 pompoms

Tissue paper in 5 different colors—10 pieces of each color, each at least 20 in. (50 cm) wide

Paper clips

Scissors

5 lengths of florist wire, each 10 in. (25 cm)

Invisible thread

1 Take a set of ten pieces of tissue paper in one color and layer them on top of each other. Mark out a rectangle 20 in. (50 cm) long and 14 in. (36 cm) wide for your biggest pompom. Hold the layers together with a few paper clips and cut out the rectangle through all the layers. Fold the layered tissue paper backward and forward into a concertina as if you were making a fan. Each fold should be about 1½ in. (4 cm) wide. Crease each fold as you make it.

2 Wrap a piece of florist wire around the center of the tissue paper a couple of times and then make a small loop to hang up the pompom. Twist the end of the wire around the base of the loop to secure it.

3 Round off each end of the tissue paper concertina by trimming it with a pair of scissors.

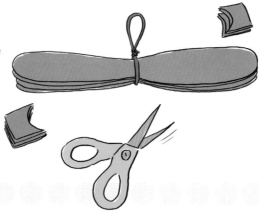

4 Open out each side of the tissue paper to make a circle, then gently lift and separate all the layers to create a full pompom shape.

5 Thread a length of invisible thread through the wire loop and your pompom is ready to hang. Repeat the steps to make five different pompoms. If you want the pompoms to be different sizes, change the width of the rectangle each time but keep the length at 20 in. (50 cm).

Garland

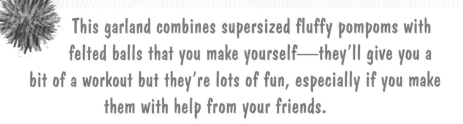

This garland combines supersized fluffy pompoms with felted balls that you make yourself—they'll give you a bit of a workout but they're lots of fun, especially if you make them with help from your friends.

You will need

Large pompom maker

Scissors

5 balls of yarn in assorted colors

¾ oz. (20 g) wool tops in 5 assorted colors, available from craft stores

J-cloth

Dishwashing detergent

Pitcher (jug) or spray bottle

8 in. (20 cm) piece of bubble wrap

Butcher's twine

Yarn needle

1 Use the pompom maker to make ten pompoms in assorted colors, then tie the middle of the pompom with a length of yarn 12 in. (30 cm) long, leaving long tails to attach to the garland. Fluff up the pompoms and trim any loose or long ends.

2 To make the felted pompoms, take a small piece of wool top and pull it out flat so there are no clumps of fibers and all the fibers run in one direction. Lay it on the J-cloth. Take another piece and do the same but lay it down with the fibers running across the ones in the first piece. Keep adding layers of wool top, criss-crossing the fibers until you have a large ball of wool tops, about 8 in. (20 cm) in diameter. Mix a small amount of warm water with a squeeze of detergent in a pitcher (jug) or spray bottle and dampen the ball of wool tops slightly.

Tip

You can make the garland with just the supersized fluffy pompoms if you don't have any wool tops, or use ready-made felt balls instead from craft supply stores.

3 Hold the ball and gently start to roll it between both hands. Do not apply much pressure at this point; the slower you start the less likely the felt will crack. Squirt on more soapy water as the wool dries and continue to roll until the ball starts to felt (stick together and thicken); it will suddenly feel smaller and harder.

4 Now put the ball inside the sheet of bubble wrap with the textured bubbles on the inside, and keep rolling the ball back and forth. This adds more friction so the ball will felt more quickly. After 5–10 minutes of rolling, your ball will be felted and ready to use.

5 Make nine more balls in the same way. Try to use the same amount of wool top each time so the balls are the same size.

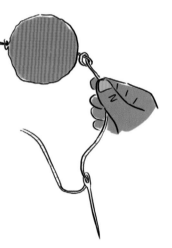

6 Thread the needle with a piece of butchers' twine 2.5 yd (2.5 m) long. Working from the center of the twine outward, thread a felt ball onto the twine by pushing the needle through the center, and tie a knot in the twine either side to keep it in place.

7 Using the yarn ends, tie a pompom tightly on the twine after the felt ball. Keep alternating felt balls and pompoms until your garland is ready to hang!

Keep on ROLLIN'!

Pompom Felt Flowers

These pompom flowers will last forever! Make a bouquet to give as a gift, or simply use them to add a splash of color and fun to decorate your room. This project uses the quick fork method to make mini pompoms.

You will need

Makes 5 flowers

Template on page 125

5 wooden skewers

Green paint and paintbrush or felt-tipped pen

Pencil or air erasable marker

5 pieces of felt in different bright colors

Scissors

3½ yd (3.2 m) yarn in 5 different bright colors.

Large fork

Yarn needle

White (PVA) craft glue

Embroidery floss (thread) in bright colors

Embroidery needle

1 Color the skewers green with the paint or felt-tipped pen and allow to dry. Copy the flower template on page 125, pin it to the felt, and draw around it twice on each color felt. Cut out the flowers carefully and place to one side in matching pairs.

2 Choose your first color yarn, cut off 8 in. (20 cm) and set aside. Take the fork and then use all the rest of that color yarn to make a mini pompom on the fork (see page 12). Use the cut-off piece to tie it in the middle, leaving the ends long.

3 Fluff up the pompom and trim any ends to make a neat ball, but do not cut off the two long tie ends because they are needed to fix the pompom to the flower. Repeat steps 2 and 3 with the other yarn colors so you have five pompoms in total.

4 Choose a pompom for each felt flower, mixing the colors. Thread one end of a pompom tie into the yarn needle and push it through the center of a felt flower piece. Remove the needle to leave the yarn end on the back. Repeat with the other pompom yarn end, bringing the needle through next to the first end.

5 Lay the flower face down with the yarn ends on top and lay the skewer down between them. Tie the yarn ends tightly together over the skewer—ask someone to help you to hold the knot in place as you tie it. Trim the yarn ends if they are still quite long.

6 Take the matching color felt flower and coat one side with a thin layer of craft glue. Stick it onto the back of the first flower for a neat finish and to hold everything together.

Variation

Why not try creating star- or heart-shaped felt flowers? Simply draw the shape you want and use it as a template to cut out the felt pieces.

7 Thread the embroidery needle with a different color of embroidery floss, knot it, and overstitch (see page 17) around the edges of the felt flower. Secure your thread at the end with a few small stitches. Repeat until all your flowers are made, then arrange them in a vase.

Make a BUNCH for a FRIEND

Hanging Pompom Heart

These pretty decorations are ideal for special occasions—a baby shower, engagement, wedding, or just to hang in your bedroom! The pompom flowers are really quick to make and you could use them to decorate any frame shape, the top of a gift box, or even a hat!

You will need

Template on page 119

Corrugated card—you could use one side of a cardboard carton

Pencil

Large scissors

Pretty gift wrap to match the tissue paper

Glue stick

Narrow ribbon, for hanging

Reel of florist's wire

Wire cutters

4 sheets of tissue paper, 20 x 30 in. (50 x 75 cm)—1 sheet of paper will make 4 pompoms

Scissors

White (PVA) craft glue

1 Copy the template on page 119 and draw a heart shape on the corrugated card. Cut out the heart shape, using large scissors. Cut out the middle section, so that you have a slim frame. Do the same with the gift wrap and use glue stick to stick the gift wrap to one side of the heart so that the back looks pretty too!

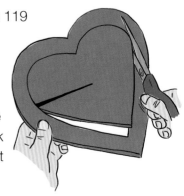

2 Make a small hole at the top of the heart and thread your hanging ribbon through the hole. Tie to secure.

3 Take two sheets of tissue paper together and fold them in half, long edge to long edge. Do this again and press the creases. Open up the paper and cut it along the creases into four long strips, each 5 in. (12 cm) wide.

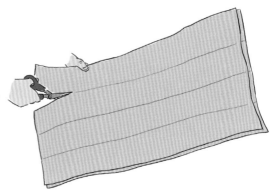

4 Take one strip (of two layers) and fold it in half, then in half again, and then in half again. Crease firmly then open it out so you see eight small rectangles. Cut along the creases. For each strip divide the rectangles into two neat piles of eight (remember the paper is double). Do the same with the other two sheets and you will end up with 16 neat piles!

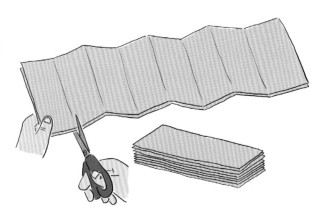

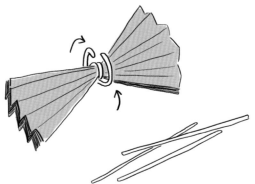

5 Cut the florist's wire into 16 equal 6-in. (15-cm) pieces with wire cutters or old scissors and put to one side. Take one pile of tissue paper sheets and fold over ½ in. (1 cm) along the shortest length. Continue making concertina folds as if you were making a fan until you get to the end of the tissue paper, then wrap a piece of florist's wire around the center of the folded strip. Twist to secure. Do the same with all the other piles.

6 Fan the paper out into a circle and then fluff the pompoms. To do this, hold the pompom at the back where the wire is twisted and gently separate the top layer on one side. Pull this as far as you can toward the center of the pompom. Repeat on the other side. Then do the same with the next layer, and continue layer by layer pulling them all forward into a nice rounded shape at the front. Trim any long pieces of wire with wire cutters.

7 Take one pompom and glue it to the middle "dip" in the heart shape, using craft glue. Place two more on either side of the first one. Continue adding pompoms, making sure that you have an equal amount on each side of the heart. Fluff up any layers that may have been flattened.

A posy of POMPOMS

Pompom Letters

Use these funky pompom initials to decorate your bedroom and make it really individual! The letters are made from a 3-D cardboard shape covered in tissue paper, then stuffed with small pompoms. Making the letters may seem a bit tricky at first but once you get the hang of it you'll soon be making the whole alphabet!

1 Pull apart your cardboard box so that it is flat and, using glue stick, glue sheets of math paper onto the cardboard. Either draw your own initial in block letters onto the squared paper or use the alphabet provided on page 116 as a guide for your chosen letter. The squares will help you to draw straight lines and right angles. Draw the letter approximately 6 in. (15 cm) tall with each of the strokes about 1½ in. (4 cm) wide.

You will need

Alphabet on page 116

Squared math paper (small squares are best)

Glue stick

Pencil and ruler

Scissors

String (for curved letters)

Cardboard from a cardboard box or carton (a shoe box is ideal)

Masking tape

Tissue paper

White (PVA) craft glue

Paintbrush

Blunt knife

Variegated yarn

Large fork

Craft pompoms in different sizes and colors

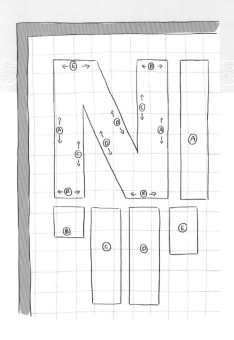

2   Measure each edge of your letter, and draw a rectangle with the same length and 1½ in. (4 cm) wide, to make the side pieces of the 3-D letter. Do this for all the outside and inside edges of the letter, then label them to help you to match up the sides—so A with A, B with B, and so on (for this letter N you would need 10 rectangles).

3   For letters with curved edges, use a piece of yarn or string to measure the curved edge. Draw a rectangle with the length to match this measurement, and 1½ in. (4 cm) wide. Measure the outside and inside edges of all the curved pieces and draw rectangles to match. Label the matching pieces.

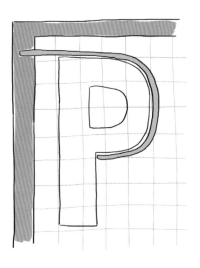

A B C D E F G
H I J K L M N
O P Q R S T U
V W X Y Z

Tip

You can also make the letter by printing out an outline capital letter in Arial Black at about 500 pt from your computer— you can then cut it out and stick it on the cardboard.

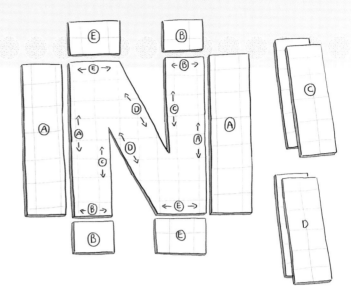

4 Cut out all the pieces of the letter—the main shape and all the sides.

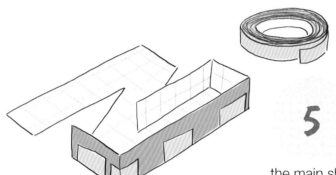

5 Match up the sides of the letter to the main shape using the letters on the templates; so A to A and B to B, and so on. Use masking tape to stick the sides to the main shape and to stick the corners together.

6 Tear the tissue paper into small pieces. Dilute the craft glue with water and then brush it over the letter, sticking the tissue paper to the surface as you go, until the letter is completely covered—back, sides, and inside. Overlap the pieces and paste tissue right across and around the joins and bends, and over the top of the edges to strengthen these and to avoid flaps of unstuck tissue paper. Push paper into the tight angles with a blunt knife. Paint all over with glue again once you have covered the box, as this will give it a nice varnish. Allow to dry.

7 Make about five mini pompoms using the fork technique (see page 12) and the variegated yarn. Using craft glue, glue these pompoms inside the letter, spacing them out around the letter. Now fill in all the gaps with craft pompoms.

8 To make a 3-D solid letter, repeat the steps above but cut out two cardboard shapes of the main letter and stick the second one on top of the sides after step 5. Cover the shape with tissue paper and stick the pompoms on top of the letter.

Tip
Using variegated yarn gives you instant multicolored pompoms. Look out for different colorways at the yarn store.

BRIGHT and DOTTY

Templates

The full size (100%) templates can be traced (see page 10) or photocopied. The half-size (50%) templates need to be photocopied at double the size, using the 200% zoom button on a photocopier. The standard templates for small, medium, and large pompoms are in the craft techniques section on page 9.

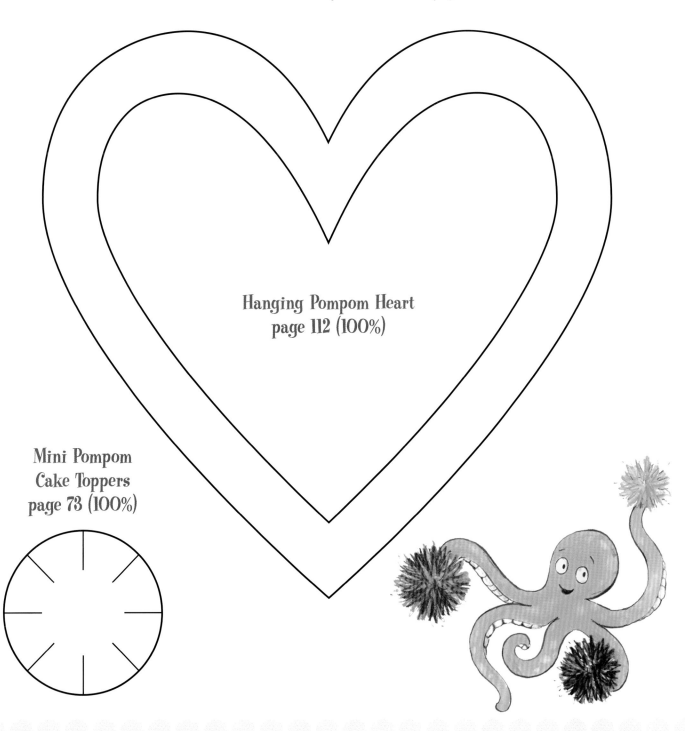

Hanging Pompom Heart
page 112 (100%)

Mini Pompom
Cake Toppers
page 73 (100%)

Tulle Birdies
page 38 (100%)

Funny Faces Hand Puppets
page 36 (100%)

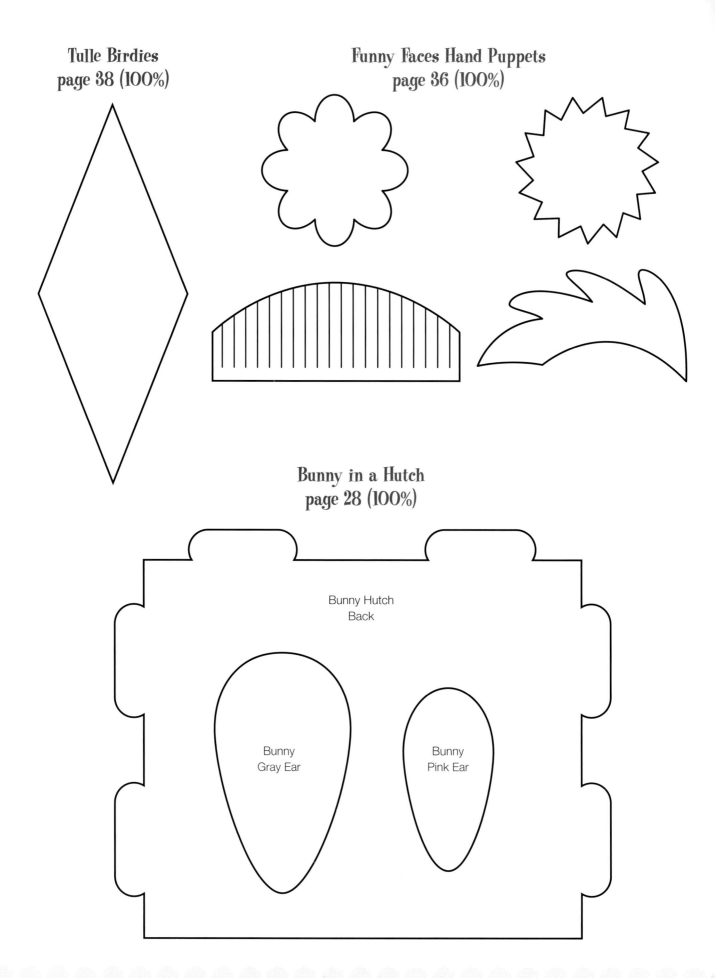

Bunny in a Hutch
page 28 (100%)

Bunny Hutch
Back

Bunny
Gray Ear

Bunny
Pink Ear

Bunny in a Hutch
page 28 (100%)

Bunny Hutch
Left Side

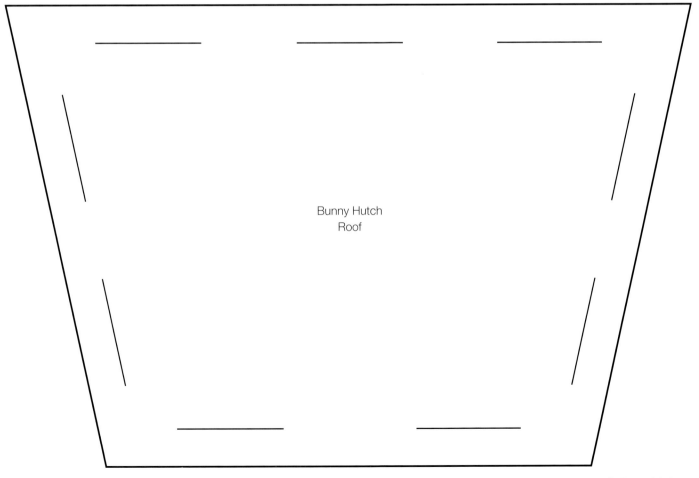

Bunny Hutch
Roof

Bunny in a Hutch
page 28 (100%)

Bunny Hutch
Right Side

Bunny Hutch
Front

Pompom Owl
page 31 (100%)

Speckled Eggs and Chick
page 70 (100%)

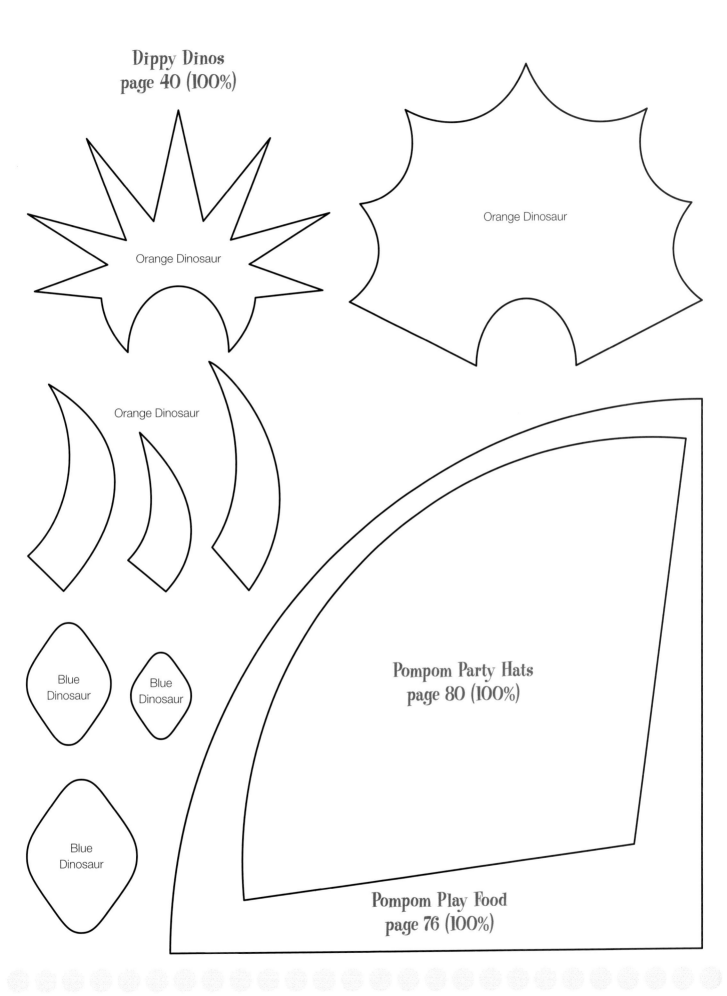

Dippy Dinos
page 40 (100%)

Orange Dinosaur

Orange Dinosaur

Orange Dinosaur

Blue Dinosaur

Blue Dinosaur

Blue Dinosaur

Pompom Party Hats
page 80 (100%)

Pompom Play Food
page 76 (100%)

Pompom Bookmarks
page 96 (100%)

Snowball Decorations
page 60 (100%)

Clothes Pin Fairy
page 64 (100%)

Easter Lamb Mobile
page 66 (100%)

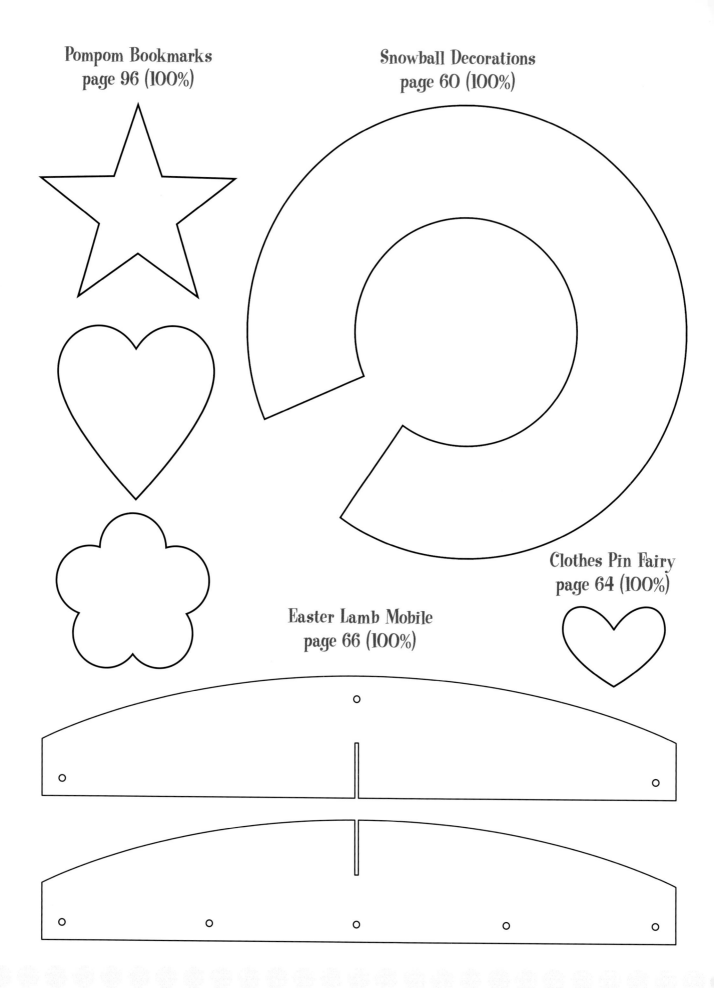

Easter Lamb Mobile
page 66 (100%)

Poodle Phone Case
page 90 (100%)

Caterpillar Bag Charm
page 86 (100%)

Pompom Felt Flowers
page 109 (100%)

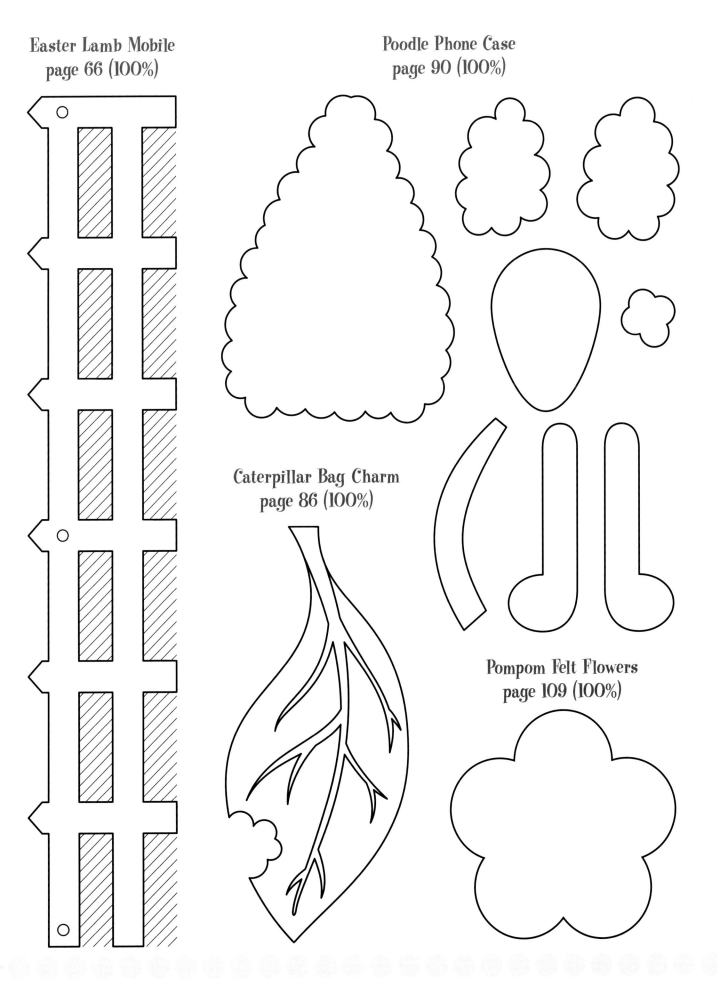

Pumpkin Wall Hanging
page 46 (50%)

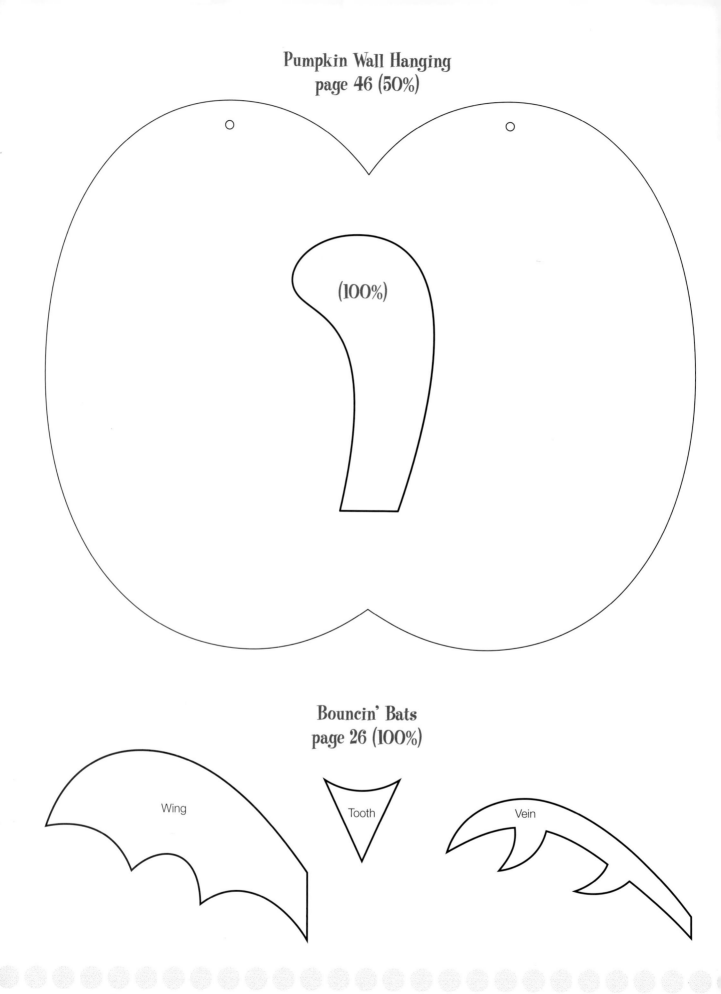

(100%)

Bouncin' Bats
page 26 (100%)

Wing

Tooth

Vein

Suppliers

Index

US

A C Moore
www.acmoore.com

Create for Less
www.createforless.com

Darice
www.darice.com

Hobby Lobby
www.hobbylobby.com

Jo-ann Fabric & Crafts
www.joann.com

Michaels
www.michaels.com

Mister Art
www.misterart.com

Walmart
www.walmart.com

UK

Baker Ross
www.bakerross.co.uk

Blooming Felt
www.bloomingfelt.co.uk

Early Learning Centre
www.elc.co.uk

Homecrafts
www.homecrafts.co.uk

Hobbycraft
www.hobbycraft.co.uk

John Lewis
www.johnlewis.com

Mulberry Bush
www.mulberrybush.co.uk

The Works
www.theworks.co.uk

Yellow Moon
www.yellowmoon.org.uk

Credits

Project makers
All projects by Lucy Hopping, unless
  stated otherwise below:
Libby Abadee and Cath Armstrong
  pp. 60-61
Juliet Carr pp. 73-75, 112-113
Sarah Fiorenza pp. 88-89
Charlotte Liddle and Friends pp. 104-105,
  109-111
Charlotte Liddle and Lucy Hopping
  pp. 106-108
Catherine Woram pp. 23-25, 52-56,
  62-63, 93-95, 100-101
Claire Youngs pp. 57-59

Photo credits
All photography by Caroline Arber unless
  stated otherwise below:
Cath Armstrong pp. 60-61
James Gardiner pp. 57-59
Jo Henderson pp. 84-85
Emma Mitchell pp. 73-75, 93-95,
  100-101, 112-113
Claire Richardson pp. 106-108
Jo Tyler pp. 104-105, 109-111
Penny Wincer pp. 88-89
Polly Wreford pp. 23-25, 52-53, 54-56